THE UNLUCKIEST ALL BLACK?

THE UNLUCKIEST ALL BLACK?

Alexander 'Nugget' Pringle
9 November 1899 – 21 February 1973

A Personal View
Compiled with the Help of a Scrapbook by
Robert Greig Pringle
His Nephew

Copyright © 2022 Robert Pringle

The moral right of the author has been asserted.

Apart from any fair dealing for the purposes of research or private study, or criticism or review, as permitted under the Copyright, Designs and Patents Act 1988, this publication may only be reproduced, stored or transmitted, in any form or by any means, with the prior permission in writing of the publishers, or in the case of reprographic reproduction in accordance with the terms of licences issued by the Copyright Licensing Agency. Enquiries concerning reproduction outside those terms should be sent to the publishers.

Disclaimer: While every effort has been made to establish the copyright owners, it has not always been possible to do so. Upon contact from a missing copyright holder, the author would be happy to include any acknowledgement of copyright in future editions of this book.

Matador
Unit E2 Airfield Business Park,
Harrison Road, Market Harborough,
Leicestershire. LE16 7UL
Tel: 0116 279 2299
Email: books@troubador.co.uk
Web: www.troubador.co.uk/matador
Twitter: @matadorbooks

ISBN 978 1803130 774

British Library Cataloguing in Publication Data.
A catalogue record for this book is available from the British Library.

Printed and bound in the UK by TJ Books Ltd, Padstow, Cornwall
Typeset in 12pt Adobe Jenson Pro by Troubador Publishing Ltd, Leicester, UK

Matador is an imprint of Troubador Publishing Ltd

Dedicated to the memory of my father,
Frank Pringle

Table of Contents

Foreword		ix
Acknowledgements		xi
List of Illustrations		xiii
Introduction		xvii
Chapter 1	A Line of Tall Timber: *Parvis e Glandibus Quercus*	1
Chapter 2	1922 Oriental and Wellington	8
Chapter 3	The Southern Tour	13
Chapter 4	1923 Annus Mirabilis: Wellington, North Island and the All Blacks	18
Chapter 5	All Black Selection – In Camp	52
Chapter 6	The Second Test	76
Chapter 7	Back to the Day Job	109
Chapter 8	1924 A Time of Trials	126
Chapter 9	1925 Annus Horribilis	204
Chapter 10	1926 Back in Action: In Search of Form and Fitness	207
Chapter 11	1927 Another Crack of the Whip – With a Broken Arm	220
Chapter 12	1928 and 1929 Brother Frank – And a Kick in the Teeth	230
Chapter 13	The 1930s, the War Years and Illness Strikes	239
Chapter 14	Recovery, Reunions, Retirement	243
Bibliography		247
About the Author		251

Foreword

It started life as a ledger, hardbacked, sturdy, and with alphabet-tabbed pages. Randomly, it would seem, were some left-facing pages ruled immaculately by hand in red ink – name of firm, date of order, amount of draft, when due, date received. There is but one completed entry, under S, in the same immaculate tiny hand, now in black ink: 'W.H. Smith & Sons, Newspapers, Jan–June 1914'. Later, the final pages were used for pencilled domestic accounts, presumably of my grandparents – items such as 'soap', 'candlestick', 'Alice dress', 'malt 4-9', 'F. Ball pants Black 5-6'.

Only much later did it become my grandmother's scrapbook, when the margins of the final accounts pages were glued together to conceal them, and newspaper cuttings of Nugget's rugby exploits from 1922 to 1924 heavily pasted in from the front. Many of the cuttings appear to have been accumulated, trimmed and stuck in at a later date.

The first few pages carry team photos and action shots on both sides, but soon we find rugby-related cuttings, match reports and illustrations confined to the right, various other items being pasted in on the left, In 1924, however, the pace quickens, and we find press cuttings and photographs stuck in on both sides once more, cheek by jowl, Every inch of space has been used, meaning that while the items are loosely grouped , they are quite out of date order, different accounts of the same match on occasion being up to three pages apart.

Occasionally the source and date of a cutting are written in ink in my grandmother's hand, but most either carry the journal's masthead and date or are undated. However, it was not difficult to identify the dates of the matches by reference to the National Library archives.

Grandmother's work ended in 1924. Later the book must have passed to Nugget, who sellotaped in a few cuttings and other items both from his Dunedin days in the war years, and his later life in Christchurch. Finally, there are a few loose cuttings of deeds of my father and cousin in later years.

The scrapbook came to me on the death of my father, and only with the Covid pandemic and the first lockdown did the idea of this biography come to me. Researching, writing and publishing it have kept my hands, mind and, to some extent, heart occupied during the first year of the pandemic, and been a joy. Almost fifty years after his death, Uncle Alex has done me one more great kindness.

Acknowledgements

I owe my thanks to Dr Ron Palenski for advice and support throughout the work's gestation, while I am grateful also for the kind assistance of the following: Alan Gray and Christine Stanley of Pauatahanui; Stephen Berg of the New Zealand Rugby Museum; John Willis of the Oriental Rongotai Rugby Club, where Nugget's All Black jersey hangs; Jude McKee of Hurricanes and Wellington Rugby; the most efficient and helpful staff of the National Library of New Zealand and of the New Zealand Defence Force Personnel Archives and Medals; thanks also to Richard Boag, of the Old Boys-University RFC and Mike Parkinson, as well as those other administrators of clubs and provincial unions who responded to my requests for help with the research. My special thanks to Stuart Hay, Photographer, for help with the illustrations. This book would not have seen the light of day without the invaluable help, encouragement and artistic skills of my son, Christopher Pringle, and the inestimable editorial skills of his wife, Glenda. Any factual errors, nonetheless, are mine and mine alone.

List of Illustrations

From the scrap-book or family archives unless otherwise stated

Title page: The Scrapbook and the Cap.
Frontispiece: Signed studio portrait.
Fig.1. The back of the cigarette card.

GALLERY A pp 6-7

Fig.2. The scrapbook.
Fig.3. Robert and Agnes Pringle.
Fig.4. Agnes Selina Wilson Greig Pringle.
Fig.5. Agnes Pringle with her sons.
Fig.6. Wellington v Taranaki 19.8.22. The team, the scrapbook and the cap.
Fig.7. Wellington v Taranaki 19.8.22. The team.
Fig.8. Shot putt trophy voucher 1923.
Fig.9. Making 120 at Newtown Park.

GALLERY B – Ories, Wellington and North Island pp 50-51

Fig.10. North Island team, 1923
Fig.11. Action v. Berhampore 28.4.23
Fig.12. Caricatures, v Otago 8.9.23.
Fig.13. Action, Wellington v Otago 8.9.23

GALLERY C – V Waratahs, First Test 1923 pp 74-75

Fig.14. Caricature, N.Z. Truth.
Fig.15. In training for the first test.
Fig.16. A cauliflower ear.
Fig.17. First test training squad.
Figs.18 & 19. Good luck and hard luck telegrams.

GALLERY D – The Second Test, 1923 pp 122-125

Figs.20 & 21. Good luck telegrams.
Fig.22. Second test All Blacks.
Fig.23. Second test Waratahs.
Fig.24. Three cheers for the All Blacks.
Fig.25. Waratah's war-cry.
Figs.26 & 27. Action from the second test.

GALLERY E pp 234-238

Fig.28. North Island 1924.
Fig.29. Nugget's nuptials 1934.
Fig.30. Officiating at the athletics 1943.
Fig.31. In uniform 1945.
Fig.32. At home with Jean.
Fig.33. Old-Timers Day with Bob Paton.
Fig.34. Nugget's jersey.
Fig.35. Nugget's Wellington cap.
Fig.36. His All Black cap.

Signed studio portrait, also the image on the cigarette card.

Introduction

The cigarette card tells the story:

Fig.1. The back of the cigarette card.

The profile by Lindsay Knight for the New Zealand Rugby Museum goes further:

'Nugget' Pringle, All Black #279

Alexander Pringle was a readily identifiable figure while playing for Wellington representative sides in the 1920s. The Oriental Club man stood about 1.96m tall, or 6ft 5 inches which was an exceptional height in those days, and probably the equivalent in modern times, with the average build having risen so much through the years, of someone around 6ft 9 or 10 inches.[1] Pringle was nicknamed 'Nugget' and was the essence of wholehearted endeavour and commitment throughout a long career. In the old 2-3-2 scrum formation he played as either a backrow forward or a lock. Obviously because of his height he was an asset in the lineouts. His bulk also made him a strong scrummager and despite his size he was surprisingly mobile in open play. After playing for the North Island in 1923 and for a combined Wellington-Manawatu-Horowhenua side against the touring New South Wales side Pringle was included in the New Zealand side which played in the second unofficial[2] test in Christchurch, scoring a try in the 34-6 win.

---

1   Nugget's height is given variously from 6'4" to 6'5½", but both the family legend and the Army medic favour the latter figure.
2   'Unofficial' as although recognised as a full 'Wallabies' international by the Australian Rugby Union (ARU), it is not by the New Zealand Rugby Union (NZRU), which did not see the NSW side as fully representative of Australia. See '1923 Waratahs tour of NZ', Wikipedia. The loss of manpower in WWI had been so great that the Queensland Rugby Union was dissolved, and it was not until 1928 that it was re-formed, and rugby union played once again in the clubs and Great Public Schools of Brisbane. A full Australian side did not play the All Blacks between 1914 and 1929.

That proved to be his only All Black appearance. He made the North Island side in 1924 again and was in the two trial matches that year. But he was overlooked rather unluckily for the side which toured Britain and France and became known as the 'Invincibles' because of an unbeaten record. Pringle had another All Black trial in 1927 before the team was chosen to tour South Africa the following year but missed selection then, too. Between 1922 and 1927 Pringle played in 26 matches for Wellington. He was in the side beaten 10-6 in a 1923 Ranfurly Shield challenge against Hawkes Bay and would have been in the side beaten 58-6 in a 1926 challenge. But on that occasion Pringle was unavailable to travel to Napier.

Lucky for Hawkes Bay!

CHAPTER 1

A Line of Tall Timber:
Parvis e Glandibus Quercus

Born and bred in Wellington, Alexander 'Nugget' Pringle was of pure, proud Scottish stock and came from a line of big men. His grandfather, William Pringle, born in 1825, emigrated with his wife Isabella, nee Oliver, from Caithness on the *Glentanner* in 1857 and settled on the Brugh's farm in the Catlins in South Otago. A shepherd, William died in 1866, somewhat ironically, a few months after having been gored by a bull. He was buried in an unmarked grave in Romohapa Cemetery, probably in his employer's family plot, and was described as being 6'2" inches in height and 'very strong'.

His son Robert, Nugget's father, was born on 27 August 1863 in Popotunoa. He left home at 13, returning some time later, according to family legend, to give his hated drunkard stepfather Robert Scott, 'a hiding' for mistreating his mother. In later years he headed for the Australian goldfields, passing through Wellington, where he met Agnes Selina Wilson Greig, born 21 February 1873. She was from Dumbarton, near Glasgow, and had emigrated as a small child with her parents and four siblings in 1876 as assisted immigrants on the *Invercargill*.[1] Failing to strike it lucky in Australia, but nonetheless lucky in love, Robert returned to Wellington, married Agnes, and settled there.

Robert stood 6'5" and was a big man. He was held in high regard as a senior overseer for the City Corporation and was presented with a tea and coffee set and silver Baumes watch and chain for his work in supervising the Melrose improvement scheme. He was something of an athlete also, tossing the caber and wrestling at sporting events in Newtown Park, and being a good rifle shot. By way of contrast, his wife was of small stature, but with an iron will, to the extent that her children grew up in considerable awe of her, if not a little fear in certain respects.

Robert and Agnes had seven children, the first of whom, Robert Oliver (b. 3 February 1893), died as a result of an accident at the age of two. Nugget (b. 9 November 1899) was the eldest boy of the surviving children, three boys and three girls. They were all of above average height, and Frank (Francis William, b. 1 October 1907), Nugget's younger brother and the author's father, stood over 6'3". He, too, played rugby for the Oriental club,

---

1. And they nearly didn't make it! Both Nugget's grandparents and his mother had hazardous journeys. The *Glentanner* was laid on her beam-ends in a storm in the roaring forties. Top-masts, jib, rigging and sails were lost, together with one crewman. As 'the masts went down' the ship righted herself and completed her journey to Lyttelton, where the master later wrote to the local paper complimenting the locals on the quality of his replacement spars. According to family legend, the *Invercargill* was blown off course and took six months to complete the voyage, two mutinies were put down and she eventually made landfall on the West Coast of the South Island, with only half a barrel of ship's biscuit and a little over a cask of water left. The legend has it that, suffering from malnutrition, little Agnes was carried ashore on a pillow. This is, at least in part, apocryphal, if only because the *Invercargill* was a fast new ship, sister ship to the *Dunedin* of frozen meat fame, and the *Otago Daily Times* of 25 September 1876 carried a very full account of an uneventful voyage from Glasgow to Port Chalmers of 90 days duration!

giving up after his nose was broken for the third time. The third son, Colin James (b. 5 January 1913), also a six-footer, was in the Oriental junior team that won the Junior 'B' Championship and Club Cup in 1933, winning an impressive 13 out of 15 games. He went on to have a distinguished career with the Poneke seniors and Wellington reps in the mid-1930s. The girls were Agnes Elizabeth (McCutcheon, b. 21 February 1894), Ellen Oliver (Wharton, b. 10 June 1897) and Alice Mary (also Wharton [Alice and Olive, as she was known, married brothers], b. 20 February 1902). Robert Sr died in 1934; his wife, ten years his junior, died more than 20 years later in 1956. The silver watch hung on the wall beside her bed to the end. It was said she kept his wrestling trunks in a drawer.

The Early Years

Alex played rugby at Wellington South School, where the headmaster at the time was George Flux, also Patron of the newly formed Berhampore Football Club.(Ref. Noble-Campbell). Others who attended school with him and went on to become well-known in rugby circles included Cliff Porter, fellow Wellington representative and later captain of the Invincibles. Nugget played initially as a 'front-ranker' and was nominated for the Wellington school reps, but he did not get in as he was too big – at the age of 13 he stood 5'10"!

He left school in 1913, aged 13 or just 14, and joined the Post and Telegraph Department (P&T), where he had no opportunity to play football as he was working on Saturdays. Apart from one or two midweek representative games, the first game of rugby he saw was, according to 'Racket'[2] ('Rapid Rise in Rugby', June

---

2 'Racket' was probably Arthur Carman, Wellington publisher, bookseller, journalist, writer and historian. Stephen Berg, New Zealand Rugby Museum, personal communication.

1939), 'the memorable battle in the mud between New Zealand and the 1921 Springboks, the final test at Wellington, which resulted in a draw'. 'Racket' continues:

> 'Nugget' was then 21 years of age, and the call of Rugby was beginning to claim him, as he had a few games that year in interdepartmental matches. The P and T played the Police and other such sides, and it is interesting to recall that the CPO Pastimes Club won the Ronaldson Cup, played for in Wellington by Public Service Teams, and in the P and T team there were 8 Wellington reps at the time.

So Nugget was in good company. And it wasn't only rugby. 'Racket' also notes that Nugget played cricket for 15 years in the senior grade of the Wellington Mercantile Cricket League for the Pastimes Club as a right-arm medium-fast bowler 'and in one game he knocked up 112'.[3]

In the scrapbook is an undated hand-drawn comic strip of seven round 'windows' by 'THP' titled 'Newtown Park – Making 120', presumably representing that innings. One window is labelled 'Pringle saw nothing but the boundary', while another depicts spectators dodging the ball. The final

---

[3] Prior to the foundation of the Wellington Mercantile Cricket League (WMCL), well-known Wellington business establishments participated in friendly inter-house matches. In 1921 they amalgamated to form the League, initially with 16 teams. Pastimes and runs by Nugget first appear in the press reports in the 1924–25 season. The WMCL proved very successful, running in parallel with, but unconnected to, the Wellington Cricket Association competitions, and by 1934–35 there were 68 teams and seven divisions. Not only that, but that season they acquired Athletic Park as a headquarters (Jennings, *Souvenir of the WMCL*, 1935). Thus it came to pass on that hallowed turf on 11 January 1936 Nugget took 5 for 28 against Taubman's on the No. 3 wicket (*Evening Post*, 10 & 13 January 1936).

window has the caged Newtown Park Zoo monkeys trying to catch it with the caption 'Keepers considering about moving monkeys'.

Newtown Park – where his father formerly tossed the caber.

Fig.2. The scrapbook.

Fig.3. Robert and Agnes Pringle.

Fig.4. Agnes Selina Wilson Greig Pringle.

Fig.5. Agnes Pringle with her sons: (l. to r.) Colin, Alex and Frank.

Fig.6. v Taranaki 19.8.22. The team, the scrapbook and the cap.

Fig.7. Wellington v Taranaki 19.8.22. Back Row: Siddells, Gair, Pringle, Shearer, Mahoney, Udy, Trapski, and Jackson. Front Row: Malfroy, McRae, Ryan (Capt.), Thomas, McHerron, Swain, and Wogan.

Fig.8. Shot putt trophy voucher 1923.

Fig.9. Making 120 at Newtown Park.

CHAPTER 2

1922 Oriental and Wellington

C.K. Griffiths, a five-eighth who played for Oriental, worked in the Post Office, and he persuaded Pringle to play for the Oriental Club. So in 1922, Pringle, who then stood 6ft 4 and 1/2 ins and weighed round about 14.10, turned out as a member of the Oriental junior fifteen's pack. Coach of that team was Bob McIlraith, but just prior to June 3 Freddy Roberts [famous All Black half back of former years] approached Nugget to play in the senior team. Pringle was a little diffident about his ability to hold his own in senior company so early in his career, but Roberts was adamant – 'you play for the seniors or not at all,' was the injunction, and thus, on June 3, – a few weeks after his entry to grade football, Nugget played his first senior game against Marist on Kilbirnie Park. ('Racket', 'Rapid Rise in Rugby', June 1939)

In fact, the *Evening Post* archives reveal that his first senior game was a week earlier, against Old Boys on 27 May, played at the same venue. This was after only four games with the Juniors from 29 April 1922. Nugget played 11 games for the Ories first team over the next two months, scoring tries against Athletic on 15 July and Old Boys on 12 August. 'Racket' continues:

> The Wellington selectors that year included 2 famous ex-All Blacks in A (Rangi) Wilson and Freddy Roberts [the third selector was the even more famous W.J. (Billy) Wallace of 1905 fame], and they were so impressed with the possibilities of the tall young Oriental packman that in his first season of rugby Pringle gained a place in the Wellington Representative side for every match in the North and South Island[1] with the exception of that against Hawke's Bay, in which Wellington lost the Ranfurly Shield, this being the beginning of the brightest era in Hawke's Bay rugby.

Hawke's Bay went on to hold the 'log of wood' for five years, until defeat by Wairarapa in 1927.

The Teams for Two Tours

According to the *Evening Post* of 31 July 1922, the three selectors chose a 'team to play Hawkes Bay at Wellington on Wednesday week, 9th August' and to make the tour to Otago, Southland and Canterbury. The XV named for Hawkes Bay

---

1   In point of fact Wellington beat Taranaki at Hawera 13-3 in an early season game on 5 July and his name is not to be found in the squad published by the *Evening Post* the previous day or in the match report of 7 July. He had to wait a little longer for representative honours.

included Pringle, with a further seven players to go on the Southern tour. A 'B' team, which was classified as a Colts team, was chosen for a tour of Marlborough, Nelson and the West Coast.

Wellington v. Hawkes Bay, 9 August 1922, Athletic Park: In Defence of the Ranfurly Shield[2]

On 5 August the *Evening Post* confirmed that Pringle was in the team to play Selwyn the following day. Oriental won 3-0, but Nugget receives no mention in the brief match report. The *Post* confirmed on 8 August that Pringle was in the starting XV for the Shield game the following day, but he is not in the line-up in their match report on 10 August. What went wrong we know not, other than that, without him, Wellington lost the Ranfurly Shield to the tune of 19 points to 9. What we do know is that Nugget was back playing for Oriental against Old Boys three days later on 12 August and scored a try in their 17-0 victory, and that he was back in the Wellington team the following week.

 ### Wellington v. Taranaki, 19 August 1922, Athletic Park

Played as a curtain-raiser to the All Blacks v. Maori match, this game was won by Taranaki 15-14. According to the *Evening Post*:

---

2 The Ranfurly Shield, the highly prized interprovincial challenge trophy, in common parlance the 'Log o' Wood', was presented to the New Zealand Rugby Football Union (NZRFU) in 1901 by the 5th Earl of Ranfurly, the then Governor-General. In 1902 it was presented to Auckland as the team with the best record that season. Their first defence was against Wellington in 1904. Wellington won. Oh, to have been there! (Although Auckland won it back the following year.)

> [A]lthough the run of the play was not of a good standard, it was punctuated with incident, and worked up to an exciting climax. Wellington took the lead shortly after the start and improved their position early in the second spell, but then Taranaki reduced the margin, and, just on the call of time pulled the game out of the fire with only a point to spare. … Credit for the win is mainly due to the visiting forwards, as well as to sound tackling. The Wellington team was not a strong one, and the play was generally of poor quality.

NZ *Truth* saw things quite differently, writing: 'The late gross carelessness of the Wellington backs [who had let in two late tries when the game seemed won] undoubtedly caused the home team to lose the game.'

The scrapbook carries photographs of the Wellington and Taranaki teams which played at Athletic Park that day.

Wellington v. Auckland, 2 September 1922, Athletic Park

Before the southern tour commenced there was time to beat Auckland 19-11 at home on 2 September. This from the *Evening Post*'s match report:

> About 8000 attended the match, but the exhibition to which they were treated was not above the ordinary, though there were instances of spectacular play, mainly of an individual character, as well as a fairly interesting period of lively interchanges in the second spell, when Auckland had improved. The strange fact about the game was that Auckland showed superiority in the play between the forwards, and consistently beat the Wellington hookers to the ball.

The team sheet has Pringle in the back row on this occasion, and to judge by the other reports, this is where he played at club and provincial level in 1922. By the following year, he was established on the side of the scrum. He rarely if ever played lock.

CHAPTER 3

The Southern Tour

The scrapbook carries pictures of play in the loss to Otago at Carisbrook, while there are match reports of this and the Canterbury game.

Wellington v. Otago, 9 September 1922, Carisbrook: Goal-kicking and a Try

'The Wellington touring team fulfilled its first engagement at Dunedin last Saturday, when it met and was defeated by Otago by 27 points to 18. There were about 12,000 spectators present' (*Dominion*, 16 September 1922). After a quarter of an hour, Otago led 19-3. 'Up to this point it was noticeable that the Wellington team were all at sea, backs and forwards both seeming lost' (ibid.). But the game evened up, and the half-time score was 22-8.

Otago scored another try on the resumption, but

> [s]tung by this reverse the Wellington fifteen took a turn at attacking, and from then on to the final whistle Otago were on the defensive. But the Blacks could only bring their score up to 18, as against the 27 points of Otago. ... [The Wellington] forward of the day was undoubtedly Pringle. His height made him invaluable in the lineout, and the way he gathered in the ball time after time was good to watch. He received a lot of attention from the Otago backs, but more than held his own. Wellington is without a goal-kicker, and Pringle was given an opportunity. His second kick, from half-way, hit the cross-bar to bounce back into the field. It was a splendid attempt. With a little practice, Pringle should be competent to take Mark Nicholls' place in the Wellington team.

The *Evening Post* two days later confirms this, and also reports that, in the second half, with the score at 22-8, 'forward ... pressure against a lamentable defence on the part of Otago [ended with] Pringle eventually picking up from ragged play and going over'. In the same journal on 16 September, 'Drop-kick', reviewing the game, concludes: 'The Blacks had some dashing forwards in Standen, King, Shearer and Pringle.'[1]

---

1   'Racket' writes that Nugget had a second attempt at goal from halfway which bounced under the bar, a newspaper headline the next day read 'Successor to Mark Nicholls Arrives', and the joke among his team-mates was that Nugget had had no previous attempts at goal, nor did he have any for the remainder of the tour. Mark Nicholls was the legendary inside back and goal-kicker who played for Wellington and the All Blacks for ten years from 1920. He moved to Auckland in 1922 and played one game for that province before returning to Wellington. He was still a hero to Wellington schoolboys in the 1950s.

Wellington v. Southland, 13 September 1922, Invercargill

Next came the match against Southland on 13 September, which resulted in a 14-3 win for the home team, 'after a good exhibition of the game. Both backs handled the heavy ball well, while the forwards provided interesting open rushes, which kept the backs busy' (*Evening Post*, 14 September 1922).

Wellington v. Canterbury, 16 September 1922, Lancaster Park

According to *NZ Truth* of Saturday, 23 September 1922:

> Canterbury's final rugby representative match of the season was played at Lancaster Park in half a gale. The Wellington visitors won handsomely as a result of their more lively tactics and superior back play. The elements were certainly treacherous, as the strong southerly blew in gusts, and the sun dipped in and out amongst the clouds, with the result that the ball was blown all ways, and flashes of strong sunshine were disconcerting. As an example of what sort of wind was blowing, when Peterson kicked off after one of the spells (four spells of 20 minutes were played) the wind was behind the ball, and carried it over the fence, just missing the members' stand. ... The defeat of Canterbury by 25 to 9 proved a nasty jar to supporters of the home team.

Pringle gets two mentions. 'A little later Pringle handed the ball to Shearer, who again crossed the line' and, in the analysis: 'Pringle was ... THE STAR PERFORMER ... amongst the Wellington pack. He played a rattling fine game.' *Boys Own Annual* stuff indeed!

The scrapbook signs off 1922 at this point, but the archives tell of two end-of-season fixtures. No sooner had Pringle returned from the South Island, than he was posted north.

Wellington v. Auckland, 23 September 1922, Eden Park: Lambs to the Slaughter

On 19 September 1922, the *Evening Post* carried this item, entitled 'Return Match with Auckland': 'In response to an application from Auckland, the Wellington Rugby Union has decided to send a Wellington representative team to play a special challenge match at Auckland next Saturday (23rd). The team will leave on Thursday, returning on Monday.' The team chosen was a young one, with six, including Pringle, from the Southern tour, and eight from the colts who had toured the West Coast, including the reserves for both tours. There were in addition four new names. By way of contrast, the following day the *Post* published the names of the Wellington team to play 'a strong team' from Manawatu-Horowhenua at Athletic Park on the same Saturday. On paper this was a much stronger team.

At Eden Park, before 4,000 people (the game was competing with 'the races and a big League attraction', according to *NZ Truth*), Wellington were cut to ribbons by an Auckland back-line including All Blacks Karl Ifwerson, Don Wright and Mark Nicholls, now on a brief sojourn in the city and sleeping with the enemy. The *Post* reported that: 'The Wellington backs showed a lamentable lack of co-ordination and were often left standing' as the home team racked up 54 points to the visitors' nil. *NZ Truth* agreed: 'Wellington, though possessing good forwards, clearly demonstrated that their backs knew nothing of combined play.'

At least the home team achieved what the *Post* on 25 September considered a lucky one-point victory, 17-16, against a 'distinctly better team … which had extremely hard lines not to win. … At the conclusion of the match the Manawatu-Horowhenua team was entertained at dinner at Barrett's Hotel by the Wellington Rugby Football Union, and later the visiting footballers were the guests of that body at Nicola's performance at the Opera House.' The manner in which Nugget's happy band celebrated their Auckland thrashing is not recorded. At least they had the Sunday in which to recover before the long return train journey on the Monday.

Wellington (Southern) v. Wellington (West Coast), 30 September 1922, Athletic Park: Lambs a-gambol

What the *Evening Post* referred to on 2 October 1922 as the 'washing-up bill' for the season was 'a test between the Wellington representative teams which went on tour in the South. ... To about 1000 spectators the players, mostly young, gave a display that was for a long period full of vim and surprisingly fast and keen for the end of a protracted season. The day was perfect, but that did not take the sting from the vigour of youth.' Such vigour, in fact, that three players – one from the West Coast and two from the Southern – played in the curtain-raiser as well! 'The players were in lively mood from the outset, and not until the energies of some were well spent was there any slackening up the pace.' The journalist thought the players 'did well', and that the experience gained by those new to senior representative football should 'lead the way towards the attainment of an improved standard next season'. For Nugget, however, further indignity was heaped on last week's humiliation as: 'The team which went to the Coast proved too good for their opponents, the forwards showing better dash and command of the ball, and the backs working together more effectively. The inside backs of the Southern team were weak in handling and indulged in too much kicking. The West Coast won by a margin of 19 points.' Final score: 31-12.

A somewhat disappointing end to a fine season.

CHAPTER 4

1923 Annus Mirabilis: Wellington, North Island and the All Blacks

The start of the 1923 rugby season saw the blinds drawn and the rugby nation in mourning. While in 1921 the All Blacks had tied the three-match series against the touring South African side with a scoreless draw in rain and mud at Athletic Park (the game watched by Nugget) they had suffered, in the middle of that series, a 0-17 thrashing at the hands of a visiting New South Wales (NSW) team at Lancaster Park. Lindsay Knight however, writing of Laurie Brownlie (player profile, New Zealand Rugby Museum), notes that the team which played NSW would be regarded today as a 'New Zealand XV' or 'New Zealand A', as only three players who were involved against the 'Boks were included in that side . Nonetheless, this had been followed by further defeat by NSW in a tightly fought series in Sydney in 1922, with scores of 26-19, 8-14 and 6-8 in the decider.

Thus, when the blinds were raised to welcome the new season it was with both a good deal of concern as well as eager anticipation of a further visit by NSW – this time for another three-match series. The outcome, one would imagine (and to judge by later headlines), had become a matter of national importance, certainly of national pride.

Nugget began the season showing the same streak of fine form he had demonstrated in 1922. His first game was for Oriental against Berhampore on 28 April. 'Berhampore won by 12 points (two tries by Hickling, try by Matheson), to 5 (try by Pringle, converted by Hickey)' (from an unsourced cutting).

Nugget went on to play in all of Oriental's fixtures until the representative season intervened. More than once, he played three games in eight days. For comment on this and the rest of his rugby year, we must return to the scrapbook. On 2 June, it was the turn of Hutt:

> **ORIENTAL BEAT HUTT**
>
>
>
> The sooner numerous passengers in the Oriental pack resolve to put some of their weight into it the sooner some of the backs will be pleased. Against Hutt last week it is not too much to say the Oriental pack was outclassed. ... The spectacle of Pringle, alone in his glory, striving to hold up the opposing pack single-handed was almost pathetic. Pringle may conceivably be an Island representative and may even wear an All Black jersey before his football days conclude; he is good and keen and there is no denying it; but he cannot hold up seven men or beat four others in the lineout. ... But Oriental won, and they won by a good piece of play by the backs, to whom the forwards would not give the ball. (*New Zealand Times*, 9 June 1923)

A somewhat cross and passionate correspondent – and perhaps an Ories supporter!! And from the *New Zealand Times* of the same date: 'Pringle is Oriental's best forward these days, his tackle being worthwhile.' It wasn't just the line-out. Nugget was a fine tackler, fast around the park, and could make and score tries. Indeed, on 9 June 1923, in a 6-12 loss to Petone, he scored both of Oriental's tries.

On 16 June, in the second half of a match in which the final score was Athletic 9, Oriental 6: 'The Orientals again concentrated on forward play, and good play by Pringle, Moffitt and King resulted in the last-named touching down. ... Pringle, tall, lithe and active, was the most conspicuous forward on the ground. He uses his brain as well as brawn and is good enough for any rep team' (*New Zealand Sportsman*, 16 June 1923).

While a week later, in the first half of Oriental's match against Varsity on 23 June, 'Wickens scored a sensational try near the corner. Pringle made a wretched attempt' (*Sport*, 23 June 1923). To be fair, the *Sport* correspondent wrote that the scorer 'dived over in the corner. Pringle missed the difficult kick'. This is one of Nugget's few recorded goal kicks after the Otago game. In this case, Oriental then appear to have given the kicking duties to Adams, whose 'kicking for Ories was a feature worth noting'. Later in the article: 'Pringle, Wickens Brown and Hume asserted themselves for Ories.' Final score: Oriental 13, Varsity 0.

Other newspapers reported on the same match:

ORIENTAL DEFEAT VARSITY

Victory can be attributed to the fine display of the Oriental forwards on a ground that was eminently to their liking. ... Pringle shone to the greatest advantage on the lineouts. Time and again he sent the ball out to his backs, but unfortunately his movements were not taken advantage of. ... On a heavy, dead ground, at Kelburn Park ... the heavy and fast Oriental pack revelled in the conditions, and it was they who carried the day. ... On the Oriental side Pringle was a tower of strength and helped a set of backs that played above average form. (*Dominion*, 25 June 1923)

And:

On the Oriental side, Pringle, who has been picked for the rep. team of course, was the outstanding forward. In the lineouts he got the ball every time through making the best use of his height. ... Amongst the Orics, Pringle stands head and shoulders above his mates. He often looks over a telegraph pole and at times has spoken to the man in the moon. Only a lad, Pringle will go far in Rugby. (*NZ Truth*, 23 June 1923)

Evidently, even then, sports reporters were given to a little hyperbole, albeit but a pale pink in comparison with the purple prose of their modern-day counterparts.

And finally: 'The outstanding player on the field was Pringle, the Oriental six foot forward. He was the centre of all movements.

With his long reach the ball was his on most lineouts, and almost simultaneously every man would push – their game was to keep play close' (*Sport*, 23 June 1923).

He played in a 5-all draw against the Wellington club on 30 June, and four days later took the field for his province in Hawera.

> **WELLINGTON LOSE TO TARANAKI**
> **HEAVY RAIN DURING THE GAME**
>
> HAWERA, 4th July. Between three and four thousand people watched the representative Rugby match, Wellington v Taranaki today. The ground was very soft, and rain fell heavily during the game, making handling the ball very difficult. ... It was a forward battle, featuring dribbling rushes, stout defence, and determined tackling, lost 3-6, Taranaki scoring the only try. Mark Nicholls was back, kicking for Wellington. ... The Nicholls brothers, Wright and Pringle, were the best of the Wellington team. (*Evening Post*, 5 July 1923)

On the Saturday he scored a try as Ories defeated Varsity once more, this time 13-3, while a 3-0 defeat of Hutt in a 'mud scramble' on 21 July was followed four days later by another representative game – this time Southland at Athletic Park.

> **SOUTHLAND GO DOWN BEFORE WELLINGTON**
> **LOCAL MEN HAVE BEST OF PLAY**
> **EXCITING BATTLE BETWEEN FORWARDS**
>
> In a game which commenced poorly, but developed into a fast, open contest, Wellington defeated Southland on Athletic Park yesterday by 30 points to 18. A crowd of about 5000 saw the match, in which the home team scored eight tries to Southland's four.[1] (*New Zealand Times*, 26 July 1923)

Relatively unimportant in the overall scheme of things maybe, but the Southland game was given a good many column inches by the *New Zealand Times*. The rugby reporters in those days were invariably anonymous, neither did they see the need to have their prose accompanied by their portrait, as today's vanity dictates, but they were clearly connoisseurs of the game, passionate and commonly parochial. Their command of English was excellent, and in both their criticisms and their praise of the play and players they showed a nice turn of phrase and resorted at times to quite jolly journalism. As an example, the report of

---

1   This game was played on a Wednesday, only three days before Wellington's Ranfurly Shield challenge against Hawke's Bay the following Saturday. Following that, there were inter-island and international matches in the offing, including Wellington v. NSW on 18 August. The rugby calendar was a busy one, with games at all levels week in and week out. In this case the Wellington side for the Shield game was unchanged from the team which beat Southland with the exception of the full-back. It certainly placed a heavy demand on the players, although this does not cause comment in the match reports. Indeed, one journalist thought the Southland game would be good practice for the challenge!

the Southland match bears quoting at some length.² The teams³ were as follows:

SOUTHLAND

Full-back: Agnew
Three-quarters: R. Oughton, Brown, Coakley
Five-eighths: Bell, Hazlett
Half: J. Oughton
Pack: J. Scott, Clark, J. Fraser, V. Fraser, White, Blick, Watson (wing)⁴

WELLINGTON

Full-back: **Wright**
Three-quarters: **Jackson, Svenson, Faber**
Five-eighths: **Tilyard, M. Nicholls**
Half: **H.E. Nicholls** (captain)
Pack: **Swain, Osborne, Duncan, Pringle, Rogers, C.B. Thomas, A. Thomas, Porter** (wing)

And the play went as follows, according to the *New Zealand Times*:

---

2   Henceforth, names in bold indicate Nugget and/or his team-mates.
3   Players' names were generally set out in accordance with the positions of the backs on the field, while the wing forward's name commonly stood alone below that of the half. Positions in the scrum were in order of packing down, though not set out in scrum formation.
4   The un-named fifteenth player was Todd in the pack!

A POOR BEGINNING

Wellington lost the toss, and kicked off against a fine sun and a fair wind. The first mid-field scrum saw Wellington penalised, and Agnew found the line in the home twenty-five, where a short tussle was ended by **Porter** lining. From the line-out Todd headed a rush down to the Wellington line, and from the ruck J. Oughton shot out to Hazlett who was brought down by **M. Nicholls.** Things looked dangerous, but both teams lacked vim, the Southland forwards looking dangerous enough, but being slow to seize openings, and frequently foiled by **H.E. Nicholls.** A kick by Bell, well followed up, saw **Wright** mull: but Wellington came safely out of the corner, some kicking by Southland ending in the leather sailing over the line from Coakley's boot, and the home forwards broke through. Two passing rushes by the Wellington backs were checked, **Svenson** being tackled once, and Bell next intercepting an infield pass by **Faber** and kicking downfield. The exchange of kicks which followed resulted in a try. **Mark Nicholls** punted and Agnew returned the kick with interest, **Porter** fielding and dropping a kick in the right position for **Swain** to gather it up ten yards out and race over. **M. Nicholls** converted.

Wellington ... 5
Southland ... 0

SOUTHLAND EQUALISE

Play was anything but lively for a spell, **Porter** and **Jackson** being called upon to stem forward rushes The visiting pack seemed to have Wellington's measure and more than held their own. Then a loose rush headed by **A. Thomas** and **Porter** gained ground until stemmed by Bell. Penalties were frequent, and there was little attempt to open play up, a tight game see-sawing on either side of half-way, with Southland having a slight edge on their opponents. They penetrated the Wellington twenty-five on a miskick by **Wright**, and following the line-out, J. Oughton secured in the face of a forward rush and was considerately allowed to walk through a bunch of five Wellington men, and passed to White, who handed on to Clark for a try beneath the posts. Agnew converted neatly.

> Wellington ... 5
> Southland ... 5

Wellington were soon on the attack from the kick. **A. Thomas**, **Pringle** and **Rogers** were in the van of a rush which carried all before it. J. Oughton went down on it in vain, and the blacks piled on top of him. Twice the Wellington backs got going, **Mark Nicholls** beating two men to make a nice opening, but **Svenson** being unable to accept his pass; then **Faber** throwing forward as he was tackled at the end of a nice rush. The home pack carried on, **Swain** and **A. Thomas** being in the van, and near the line the latter was obstructed when a score was certain, the referee awarding a penalty try. **M. Nicholls** failed to convert.

> Wellington ... 8
> Southland ... 5

SWAIN SCORES AGAIN

Southland were in and around the Wellington twenty-five from now on, but the game was half-hearted, and they could not get through. Agnew once essayed a shot from a scrum infringement; he kicked a poster, but there had been a man in front in any case. It was now, after a prolonged spell in defence, that the home rearguard commenced to throw the ball about. **F. Tilyard**, in a brilliant run, on one occasion penetrated right up to the visitors' line but failed to let the ball out. **Pringle** contributed largely to the next try, which followed another slashing forward rush, **Swain** again being handy at the right moment, and scoring near the corner.

> Wellington ... 11
> Southland ... 5

Wellington soon scored again to make it 14-5, before:

> **WHITE'S FINE TRY**
>
> Southland's next score came immediately. A solo dribbling rush right from the half-way kick ended in White booting over the line and falling upon the ball for a fine try. Agnew's kick was a poor one.
>
> > Wellington ... 14
> > Southland ... 8

There was no further score before half-time, shortly before which the Southland half, J. Oughton, went off, and the back line was rearranged. In the second half:

> The Southland forwards made a brief visit to home territory from the kick until a loose rush by the Wellington forwards went the greater distance of the field. ... Wellington were kept out only momentarily by a penalty against them, a forward rush seeing **Duncan** and **Rogers** go downfield together, the Poneke man receiving a pass and running round between the posts while both teams looked on. **M. Nicholls** goaled.
>
> > Wellington ... 19
> > Southland ... 8

HOME TEAM TOO GOOD

It was only a moment before Wellington scored again. A Southland rush was checked by **Porter,** the Southland men letting him up, for which kindness he retaliated by running through the whole team. **M. Nicholls** took his pass, scored between the posts, and converted it, with a free charge.

Wellington ... 24
Southland ... 8

Southland pressed at once, Hazlett and Cosgrove working together, and Coaksey snapping up, to come to earth in the corner. **A. Thomas** was instrumental in clearing. The Southland forwards, White and Clark, worked with R. Oughton for a good rush, which was checked only by **Porter** giving a penalty away. [No yellow cards in those days!] White's kick was unsuccessful, and **Mark Nicholls** found the line. Immediately following the lineout, Wellington scored again. The **Nicholls brothers** handled, and **F. Tilyard** ran through, handing on to **Duncan** at the right moment for the lock to dash over. **Porter**'s kick missed.

Wellington ... 27
Southland ... 8

AN OPEN GAME

Play now became fast and open, both sides being willing to throw the ball about, but their backs' handling being very far short of perfection. Wellington missed more opportunities because of this fault. ... The Wellington forwards were now proving too much for the opposition. ... [But more] bad passing and faulty handling by Wellington missed chances. **Svenson, Jackson** and **Faber** all failed to accept passes which might have ended in a score, and Southland swung into the attack. Bell kicked past the Wellington backs, beat them to the ball, and sent on to R. Oughton to pass infield to Brown, the forward going over the line in the arms of **M. Nicholls** and **Faber**. Agnew converted.

Wellington ... 27
Southland ... 13

DUNCAN ONCE MORE

Give-and-take play followed [until] **Duncan** burst through near the Wellington twenty-five, sent on to **Rogers**, to **A. Thomas**, who scored at the corner. **M. Nicholls**'s kick went close.

Wellington ... 30
Southland ... 13

The Southland backs were now throwing the ball about well, but could get nowhere, and after a short-lived rush, **Duncan** battled through once more, **Jackson** carrying on, but the wing-three-quarter[5] kicked infield, Agnew played the ball, and **Jackson** ran off-side, the penalty saving the southerners.

A LAST-MINUTE SCORE

A series of scrums saw Southland clear, and the failure of several attacking movements by the Wellington backs saw Brown conspicuous in a rush in which the ball went over the line with L. Oughton on top of it, but Southland were called back for an infringement. ... With the timekeeper looking at his watch, the Southland half swung the ball out, and a good piece of passing ended in R. Oughton going into touch in the arms of **Faber**. The visiting forwards pushed ahead, Blick securing, being tackled, and 'rabbiting'[6] the ball over the line. A try was awarded, and Agnew goaled at length, the bell going at once with the score:

> Wellington ... 30
> Southland ... 18

---

5 In those days of the 2-3-2 scrum formation, the eighth forward was listed in the team-sheet as 'wing' – the wing-forward – and the wingers of today as 'three-quarters' (together with the centre three-quarter).

6 'Rabbiting ... a try was awarded.' Was rabbiting legal then, or was this a parochial Wellington journalist's oblique criticism of the referee's decision?

As for Pringle's contribution, the following appeared in the *New Zealand Free Lance*'s report:

> **WELLINGTON FORWARDS GOOD**
>
> Southland came north with the reputation of having a great forward team, probably one of the best in the Dominion. The fact that they were without J. Richardson, the New Zealand representative, undoubtedly made a big difference to them, for, although they did well, most of the time, they were no match for the Wellington forwards, especially in the loose rushes.
>
> There was a time in the Empire City when we prided ourselves on our tearaway forwards, who were wont to carry all before them in the loose, and brushing aside backs who attempted to stop their progress. I have many times drawn attention to the falling-away of recent years of the dribbling forward, but a few more displays like those given on Saturday afternoon will make me a lot more cheerful. Swain, Duncan, the brothers Thomas, and Pringle all performed in a manner to cause me to rejoice, and I feel that the future of Rugby football in Wellington is all right so far as the forwards are concerned.

And for the last word, this from *NZ Truth* of Saturday, 28 July 1923: 'In the line-outs Pringle's length was invaluable, and he played an honest, strenuous game, fully justifying his inclusion in the North Island pack.' Indeed, as we learn in the same issue, the North Island team for the following weekend's inter-island derby had been announced. This annual fixture, first played in 1897, was always hard-fought, and commonly seen, as in this case with NSW soon to arrive and the 1924 tour of the British

Isles in the offing, as a trial prior to selection of the All Black team.

> **INTER-ISLAND GAME**
> **TEAMS REVIEWED**
> **NEW BLOOD BROUGHT TO LIGHT**
>
> In regard to the forwards, the rule of picking new blood has been departed from, probably on account of the necessity for proved metal to stand up against the heavy pack coming from the south. M. Brownlie, A. West and Jacobs have all donned All Black jerseys, while Quinton Donald, of Wairarapa has been a North Island rep. before. … Pringle of Wellington has been selected, and deservedly so.

IN SEARCH OF THE SHIELD:
THE BATTLE OF NAPIER, 28 July 1923

The same evening of the match the *New Zealand Times* contained the following report of the game in Napier:

> **WELLINGTON DEFEATED**
> **HAWKE'S BAY HOLD THE SHIELD**
> **NORTHERNERS VICTORIOUS IN FORWARD BATTLE**
> **HOW THE GAME WENT**
>
> Six thousand people were present when M. Brownlie led the Hawke's Bay team on the field. They were fifteen men of splendid physique, the Brownlie brothers being the biggest, and Mill, the half-back, the smallest. The Wellington men, uneven in height, looked weak by comparison, when **H.E. Nicholls** led them on, but they were to show that what they lacked in beef was made up for in brains.

The teams were as follows:

>  **HAWKES BAY**
>
> Full-back: Yates
> Three-quarters: Grenside, Kirwan, Mapu
> Five-eighths: Nepia, Paewai
> Half: Mill
> Forwards: Gemmell, Walker, M. Brownlie, McNab, C. Brownlie, Kirkpatrick, Irvine, Smith (wing)

WELLINGTON

Full-back: **Corner**
Three-quarters: **Jackson, Svenson, Faber**
Five-eighths: **Tilyard, M. Nicholls**
Half: **H. Nicholls**
Forwards: **C.B. Thomas, A. Thomas, Pringle, Duncan, Rogers, Osborne, Swain, Porter** (wing)

And the match report from the *Times*:

WINNING BY WEIGHT

Hawke's Bay won because of the superior weight of their forwards. Their pack has been called the best in New Zealand. It may be the finest in physique, but it has a lot to learn about forward play, and as a matter of fact, some of the biggest, notably C. Brownlie, were more of a hindrance than a help. Nevertheless, it was the strength and aggressiveness of its forwards that decided the game.

The Hawkes Bay captain kicked off against a strong breeze, but Wellington for a time were able to make no headway against the tremendous assault of the defenders, who pushed their way up the field in mass formation, reminiscent of the Springboks. ... [Eventually] 'the Wellington backs, passing accurately for the first time, gave **Jackson** a chance. He got the ball at the top of his speed, raced past Kirwan, and had three yards to go, when Yates flung himself at his heels, and threw him into touch. It was a magnificent run, eclipsed by a wonderful tackle.

[Wellington continued on the attack until] Kirwan missed **Svenson**. Mapu found himself with two men to tackle. **Faber** ran in easily near the corner to score a well-deserved try. The angle and the wind were too much for **M. Nicholls**.

[Thus, at half-time, Wellington led 3-0.]

HAWKE'S BAY SHOW THEIR METTLE

Having kept Wellington's score down to three points with the wind against them, Hawke's Bay were expected to do great things in the second spell [but Wellington defended stoutly] the Wellington forwards, particularly **C. Thomas** battling magnificently. [Ultimately, however,] Yates, fielding (a clearing kick) at half way, ran a few yards and potted a magnificent goal right between the posts. The crowd rose and cheered for half a minute.

Hawke's Bay ... 4
Wellington ... 3

WELLINGTON RETALIATE

At this critical time, when Hawke's Bay were expected to overrun the opposition, **Porter** and **C. Thomas** played like men possessed, following the ball everywhere, even kicking it out of the hands of the Hawke's Bay backs. Their example gingered up the whole team, and presently from a line-out, the ball went to **Jackson**, who was collared and lost it, but three forwards carried it over, and **Duncan** scored. ... **Mark Nicholl**'s kick went low.

>Wellington ... 6
>Hawke's Bay ... 4

The wind had died down, and it appeared as if Wellington would hold their advantage, but [they] were penalised, and Nepia, from two yards past half-way, found dead centre between the posts.

>Hawke's Bay ... 7
>Wellington ... 6

This decided the game. For twenty minutes or more Wellington had to defend continuously. ... From a lineout the Hawke's Bay backs gave Mapu a chance, **Svenson** tackled him, got the ball, and kicked in-field, right into Kirkpatrick's hands. He marked and took a shot, and there was no doubt about this goal either.

>Hawke's Bay ... 10
>Wellington ... 6

And this was the final score. The correspondent concluded:

> **CONDITIONS FAVOURABLE**
>
> Mr Bert McKenzie, of Carterton, kept strict control of a hard game, and although penalties were frequent, his judgment was sound. All but a handful of the spectators had come to see Hawke's Bay win, and they were noticeably sparing of applause for good play of the Wellington men. The ground was in good order and except for the wind conditions were as good as could be desired. The usual dinner was held after the match, when Mr E. Perry congratulated Hawke's Bay on retaining the shield. On Sunday the teams went on a motor drive, and were entertained by Mrs M.A. Perry, of Otatara. The Wellington team return on Monday.

As for Nugget: 'Every credit must be given to the forwards for their fight against such odds. The wonder is they lasted so well. ... Pringle got a hard knock early in the game and showed less dash and enterprise afterwards.' Although elsewhere: 'The Wellington forwards all played well, Varsity Thomas, Duncan and Pringle in particular' (*New Zealand Free Lance*, 1 August 1923). And 'Porter ... justified himself by playing the best forward game of the day. Pringle and Duncan were runners-up, and the whole pack, with the exception of Rogers, played well. [Alas poor Rogers – it is all in the eye of the beholder.] The forwards although lacking weight, held the scrums well. ... They also showed pace in the loose and at times took a lot of stopping. These rushes were usually led by Pringle and B. Thomas. (*New Zealand Sportsman*, 4 August 1923). There is an unattributed and undated[7] detailed account by M.E.W.[8] telling a similar story: 'The forward loose work was great, Pringle, Porter, Duncan, Swain and Rogers [Rogers redeemed!] excelling in combined footwork. ... Mr Bert McKenzie refereed the game as only a McKenzie can. Those chaps know the game from A to Z and we are lucky to have them in the game.'

An interesting note from 'Tackler' in the same issue regarding injuries sustained against Hawke's Bay includes the following:

---

7   Although this would appear from the archives to be the 4 August 1923 issue of NZ Truth.
8   Readers of NZ Truth in 1923 were spoilt for choice between the passionate accounts of 'Tackler' and the lengthy, well-written and well-informed contributions of 'M.E.W'. On 4 May, the latter wrote one headed 'Sound Advice from an Old All Black', which, together with his references to the years 1901–04, renders it virtually certain that he was Morris Edwin 'Morrie' Wood (All Black #91), an outstanding five-eighth and all-round athlete.

> 'Ginger' Nicholls has returned from Hawke's Bay with many scars and a badly swollen shoulder … no bones were broken. The bruising is particularly severe, though, and will prevent the half from playing [for Wellington] today [i.e., a week later]. Picking the ball off the toes of the big Hawkes Bay pack, 'Ginger' took a bit of knocking about before the shoulder injury sent him off. A minute before the final bump 'Gin' landed a crack on the side of the head from the elbow of Cyril Brownlie, and this was a steadier for a while. 'Gin' was just a bit dazed still when the same Brownlie's sixteen stone and the half came into violent collision. The Wellington half landed on the point of his shoulder and off he went. Cyril Brownlie's methods got him cautioned a couple of times during the match. One occasion was when he mistook Pringle's head for the ball and let loose a speculator. [This is presumably the 'hard knock' mentioned in the *New Zealand Times* report above.] This Brownlie, it might be added, has been twice ordered off the field this year. He's a valuable forward to his side, though, and it doesn't do to disqualify sixteen-stone guardians of a trophy as precious as the Ranfurly Shield.

Remarkably sporting, you might think, from a Wellington supporter!

NORTH ISLAND V. SOUTH ISLAND,
Saturday, 4 August 1923: Ear Trouble

The lanky North Island forward Pringle came on to the field on Saturday with his head in a sling [sic]. 'Nugget'[9] stopped a nasty one on the left ear in the Hawke's Bay match and that organ was so swollen that the union doctor would not let him play without it being covered by a bandage. (*NZ Truth*, 11 August 1923)

The following are some quotes from the match reports in the *New Zealand Times* of 6 August 1923:

---

9   This is the first reference to him by the press as 'Nugget', although the nickname is used freely henceforth. As a boy, the author was given to believe that his uncle joined the army to get fitter for rugby and was called 'Nugget' because his footwear was so highly polished. The two things may or may not be connected and the author cannot vouch for the truth of either. See discussion of his army career in Chapter 13.

**INTER-ISLAND TEST MATCH DRAWN
GREAT STRUGGLE ON MUDDY GROUND
WELLINGTON AND WAIRARAPA DRAW
NEW ZEALAND TEAM CHOSEN**

NORTH ISLAND (in black)

Full-back: **Stewart**
Three-quarters: **Grenside, Potaka, Peina**
Five-eighths: **Johnston, F.T. Tilyard**
Half: **Mill**
Forwards: **Bevan, Irvine, Patterson, Pringle, Righton, M. Brownlie, Gemmell, Jacob** (wing)

SOUTH ISLAND (in white)

Full-back: Sinclair
Three-quarters: Steel, Mackereth, Snodgrass
Five-eighths: Page, Bell
Half: McCarthy
Forwards: McCleary, McMeeking, Williams, Peterson, R. Stewart, Snow, G. Stuart, Knox (wing)

And from 'Tackler':

> **GREAT FORWARDS IN THE MUD**
>
> Played under conditions that are almost indescribable, the North v. South game at Athletic Park, Wellington, on Saturday ended in a draw, each side being credited with two tries. The curtain-raiser[10] which was played on the southern portion of the ground had converted that part of the playing area into a quagmire, while the northern half of the ground was mostly under water. ... A great forward struggle was looked for, and, with their heavy cavalry, the South were expected to carry the day. ... There was no disappointment over the forwards' display. It was a gigantic fight; science was thrown to the four winds and brawn took charge.

Elsewhere in the *Times*, other correspondents noted: 'A few minutes after the match began the black jerseys of the North players and the white of the South were approximately similar in colour – a dull grey.' No doubt it soon became difficult to identify players, leading to some confusion among the correspondents concerning North's first try.

---

10 That is, the Wellington Wairarapa match referred to in the headlines. It is hard to believe today that before a match of this importance in appalling conditions the decision was taken to go ahead with a senior rep. curtain-raiser across half the ground, but it seems this was the case.

>  A sweeping rush by the northern pack commenced the next movement. ... **Tilyard** and **Pringle** were instrumental in pushing the attack on. ... **Pringle** picked up and cross-kicked to **Peina**. The wing took the ball at the top of his speed and shot across the line in a good position. **Jacob** kicked a poster.

The *Dominion* of 6 August carries two versions – in the introduction: '**Grenside**, obtaining the ball ... cross-kicked to **Peina**' (who scored), but in the narrative account: '**Pringle** emerged with the ball and cross-kicked for the line. The leather was smartly snapped up by **Peina**.'

'Tackler' saw things differently: '[J]ust outside the South 25, a cross-kick by **Righton** found **Peina** alert and his vis-vis out of position.' It would seem that, in all fairness, we can on the balance of probability, award the cross-kick to Pringle as another string to his bow. That made the score: North Island 3, South Island 0.

The *Dominion*'s match report continues:

The pace was now a veritable 'cracker', and an indication of the ground can be gleaned from the number of stoppages for the removal of mud from the players' eyes. The North vanguard carried all before them in one sweeping onslaught, but they had reckoned without McCarthy, who was playing the defensive half-back game as few half-backs know how. The Southerners launched a counter-offensive, and through the agency of McCarthy and Snodgrass play was carried into opposition territory. A spirited struggle took place on the line and Williams brought the scores level by dropping over. Sinclair failed with the kick.

>North Island ... 3
>South Island ... 3

Five minutes later South repeated the performance. Snodgrass received the ball from Mackereth, and cleverly cut in between **Johnston**, **Peina** and **Stewart**, and by dint of mere speed reached the line just as **Jacob** dived at him and dragged him over. Again Sinclair had hard luck with the kick.

>North Island ... 3
>South Island ... 6

> Just before the spell closed the spectators were treated to exhibitions of line-kicking by Steel and Page, which illustrated the fine art to which the amended rule has been reduced in the South Island. Page's kick was nicely timed and placed the team in a good attacking position, from which the Blacks just managed to extricate themselves, but the kick taken by the Southern skipper travelled 65 yards before it bounced out. It was a difficult matter to distinguish between Black and White when the teams trooped off the field at half-time.

'Tackler' again: 'Half-time and a very tired 30 men left the field. Both teams stopped to a jog in the second half and of the two the South seemed to be the more tired. This was especially the case in the last 15 minutes.' No 'tactical substitutions' in those days!

According to *The Times*:

> North were soon in the attack in the second spell. … Bad as conditions had been in the opening half they became infinitely worse now. During the long spell in which the southerners were pent up in their own half of the field the ground was churned up until it became nothing but a sea of mud, in which the ball was frequently lost to the sight of the battling forwards. The spectacle of half a dozen men lumbering round in the slush and seeking vainly for the leather was frequent, and the players, North and South alike, merged into one dingy brown in which it was oftentimes utterly impossible to distinguish one side from the other.

The *Dominion* again:

> **A GREAT TRY**
>
> The dying stages were reached before North equalised with the greatest try of the day. From a scrum in midfield **Mill** whipped out the ball to **Tilyard** who transferred to **Grenside** who beat his man and passed in-field to **Mill**. The Black half had a clear run in and perfected the movement he initiated by touching down under the posts. Sinclair, the White full-back, who was playing a splendid defensive game, tackled him.

The *Times* wrote that Mills had 'tried the blind-side near the half-way line'. Having regained the ball from Grenside, Mills 'gaining sure footing in the quagmire, he went straight for the line, and crossing it, fought his way to near the goal-posts and scored.' Sadly for North Island, 'with the result of the match depending on a fairly easy kick **Jacob** missed'. 'Fairly easy'? Exhausted, with tired legs, in a sea of mud with a sodden leather ball – and no tee of course. Perhaps this was a trifle unfair to poor Jacob. 'There was little more of moment, as the end was not far distant', and the final score was: North Island 6, South Island 6.

According to 'Tackler', 'the North pack played a great game … in the second half they played the South at their own game – *en masse* formation, and what is more, beat the whites at it. … **Righton, Pringle, Brownlie** and **Gemmell** were the pick of the pack, the last-named showing out most.' And the *Times* opined that: 'Of the northern forwards **Gemmell, Pringle** and **Righton** were the most consistent workers all through, all working hard in the loose, and **Pringle** and **Patterson** starring in the lineout.'

Myths and Legends

Such a titanic struggle could not but go down in history, of course, and it was recalled by Tom Fleming in an article on inter-island games almost 40 years later ('Tom Fleming on Rugby', 1960). His résumé was correct in all but one respect, and that is when he wrote: 'It was a typical Athletic Park day with the elements combining to lift the players off their feet.' It was an appalling quagmire, and raining, but Windy Wellington is not always so, and the *Times* account is of 'a very slight breeze'. Rather than being 'lifted off their feet', the players were in fact stuck in the mud.

Fleming's erroneous assumption is understandable. What constitutes 'a gentle breeze' to a Wellingtonian may be a gale to a stranger. On the same ground, on 5 August 1961, 38 years and one day later, the author had the privilege of sitting exposed in the new Millard stand watching the All Blacks play France when the wind really was blowing. On that occasion it was rain and wind – a southerly gale, 80+ mph, with a top wind speed of 137 kph recorded at the airport. A crowd of 60,000 was expected but because of the conditions only 35,000 turned up!

It was an equally enthralling and even more legendary game, virtually the whole match being played in the northern 25 with lineout throws and passes invariably blown off course. The first half, with the All Blacks playing into the wind, was scoreless. With 15 minutes to go, the French, courtesy of their winger Dupuy, scored a length-of-the-field try against the wind and run of play to lead 3-0. Two or three minutes later, following a French heel near their line, Kelvin Tremain launched himself off the side of the scrum to gather the French full-back Lacaze's attempted clearing kick and score near the corner. Don Clarke kicked his attempted conversion parallel to the 25, and the southerly gathered the ball and carried it between the posts for a final score of 5-3 to the All Blacks.

God on that day was a New Zealander and the author was there to see it. Sadly, Uncle Alex wasn't. No doubt he was listening in on his wireless at home in Christchurch, the playing conditions all too familiar to him. The New Zealand skipper, Wilson Whineray, had the final word when he reputedly said the same drops of rain were going between both sets of goalposts.

ORIES, WELLINGTON AND NORTH ISLAND

Fig.10. North Island team, 1923. "Back Row – L.Righton, A.West, A. Pringle, W.(sic) Brownlie, B.Grenside. Standing – T.Bevan, S.Gemmell, Q.Donald, R.Patterson, W.Irvine, W.Potaka. Sitting – J.Mill, T.Peina, A.J.Griffiths (manager and selector), H.Jacob, A.Guy (selector), A.Stewart, H.Hall. In front – F.J.Tilyard, D.Johnson."

Fig.11. Action v Berhampore 28.4.23. "A line-out, showing Oriental's high reach." Are those Nugget's hands to the ball?

Fig.12. Caricatures, v Otago 8.9.23

Fig.13. Action, Wellington v Otago 8.9.23.
"The lengthy Pringle fending off Holden, Otago's half-back."

CHAPTER 5
All Black Selection – In Camp

According to 'Tackler': 'Immediately after Saturday's big game the New Zealand selectors went into committee. After due consideration' they announced the names of 20 players, including Pringle, from whom the test team was to be 'decided a few days before the game' (against NSW in Dunedin three weeks thence).

> It is to be hoped that on this occasion there will be a little more control over players than was evident in the first and second tests with the Springboks two years ago. For those two important fixtures social engagements were thought more than training, and it was only when honours were even that the New Zealand Union woke up to the fact that their representatives were a very unfit combination and so Day's Bay was ordered.[1] And there all preparations were made for the deciding test, and the team that took the field on that memorable Saturday were as fit as it was possible for man to make them.

'Tackler' continued: 'Dunedin is famed for its hospitality but there is not one case on record where hospitality has won a test match, so it behoves the New Zealand Union to get busy and pick a spot, out of town, to house the members of the team while they are undergoing training operations.' And so they did. There is, in the scrapbook, a photograph of Nugget in his All Black jersey and casual trousers seated on a chair out of doors, below which he has written 'In camp, Brighton Dunedin 1923'. 'Tackler' concluded by naming his chosen XV, which included Pringle.

The prospects of the training camp and his first cap did not prevent him from playing for Wellington against Canterbury on

---

1 For some days prior to the Third Test against the 'Boks in 1921, and the night after it, the All Blacks lodged at the Bay View Boarding House, Mrs Agatha Downes, Prop. Subsequently, this good lady sued the NZRU for damages, complaining of the players' gargantuan appetites, and their boisterous behaviour during and after the crayfish supper she hosted the evening after the game. Her claim met with limited success. For an amusing account of the proceedings at the Wellington Supreme Court, and Sir John Salmond's judgement, see 'A Rugby Rag', *NZ Truth*, 10 and 17 June 1922.

11 August or against the tourists on 18 August – a week before the first test. The *New Zealand Sportsman* (11 August 1923) reported on the Canterbury match as follows:

CANTERBURY 8 v. WELLINGTON 6[2]

WELLINGTON

Full-back: **Malcolm**
Three-quarters: **Svenson, M. Nicholls, G. Gibson**
Five-eighths: **F. Tilyard, E. Roberts**
Half: **H.E. Nicholls**
Forwards: **Swain, Osborne, Duncan, Pringle, Rogers, A. Thomas, C.B. Thomas, Porter** (wing-forward)

CANTERBURY

Full-back; J. Harris
Three-quarters: A. Fitzgerald, I.H. Brown, W. Ford
Five-eighths: R. Evans, M.L. Page
Half: A. St George
Forwards: Diedrich (wing-forward), S. Hooper, C. Greatbatch, R. Masters, L. Petersen, D. Sergison, Parker, O. Turpin

---

2   Although the game was played at Athletic Park.

The sun was making a gallant effort to break through, but a biting southerly that blew across Athletic Park made things none too pleasant for the 6000 spectators who had mustered to see this match. [There's that breeze again – but it reads as a very exciting game.] The ground was in a very bad state[3] and had not improved much from the previous Saturday. Wellington won the toss and elected to play with the wind behind them. The visitors attacked, but **Svenson** getting in a good kick, put the blacks in a safe position and **Gibson** centred nicely, and Canterbury were compelled to force down. A free kick to the blacks saw **M. Nicholls** make a good attempt to goal from near half-way. [Wellington continued to attack, but] from a passing bout by the backs Brown intercepted and made a good run, transferring to Ford when he reached **Malcolm,** giving the visitors' wing three-quarter a clear run in. Brown goaled.

> Canterbury ... 5
> Wellington ... 0

---

3   The state of the ground was not helped by a curtain raiser, virtually the final of the 5th Class Championship, in which Wellington College defeated Petone 3-0. Nugget's brother Frank kicked the winning goal.

The blacks were fighting hard to get through. **Gibson** had an unsuccessful shot from a penalty. **Teddy Roberts** was exerting his arts to make an opening for the blacks but full advantage was not being taken of them. ... From a mark '**Ginger Nicholls**' tried to add three points, but his kick met no better fate than his predecessor's. **Porter** was playing a great game at wing forward ... (eventually) a free kick enabled **M. Nicholls** to pilot the ball safely over with a good kick.

> Canterbury ... 5
> Wellington ... 3

Brown, the visitors' centre three-quarter, was proving himself the best of their backs, and he was putting in a tremendous amount of defending for his side. ... Another attack by the blacks saw **Porter** get possession and forge his way over with two Canterbury players hanging on to him. **Malcolm** made a good attempt from a difficult angle.

> Wellington ... 6
> Canterbury ... 5

The visitors made several good rushes but the superb defence of the local backs proved too hard for them to get through... From a scrum **H.E. Nicholls** worked the blind side and **Thomas** was nearly over, Harris clearing. Half-time sounded with Wellington on the attack.

On resuming the hopes of the visitors' supporters rose as they now had the assistance of a fairly strong breeze. [Again the breeze! Play swept back and forth] a fierce rush by Canterbury [then the] Wellington forwards ... made a run the whole length of the field, but the reds were not to be outdone, and they forced play back, the ball being kicked out from the ruck, and was smartly snapped up by Ford, who dived over. Brown's kick was a poor attempt.

Canterbury ... 8
Wellington ... 6

Play now became pretty brisk [What have we had until now? It is like the wind-breeze issue – all things are relative!] and the home team were kept busy defending. ... The local backs got going in some nice passing bouts, but their efforts were not of much use; there was not enough cutting-in to make the openings. Canterbury kept the upper hand in the forwards until the finish of the game and left the field with a well-earned victory.

Mr T.A. Fielding ably controlled the game. ... The Wellington pack were a determined, hard-working lot – not one weak player among them. **Pringle** was perhaps the best, and **Swain** and **Duncan**, with **C.B. Thomas**, were not far behind. **Osborne, A. Thomas** and **Rogers** never let up and supported their confreres admirably.

The Pipe-Opener, 18 August 1923: At War with the Waratahs

The NSW Rugby Union was formed in 1874, adopting the name Waratahs after the brilliant red state flowers, and a strip of Cambridge Blue jersey and dark blue shorts. It has a long and proud history. The team's first inter-state game was against Queensland in 1882, and its first visit to New Zealand took place later the same year when the side was beaten 7-0 by Auckland in the first match of a seven-match tour that did not include an international. Its first match against New Zealand was played in Sydney on 31 May 1884, the opening game of a series won 3-0 by the New Zealanders.

The first international between Australia and New Zealand was played in Sydney on 15 August 1903, before 30,000 people. On that occasion New Zealand won 22-3. In 1907 the same event attracted a record 52,411 spectators. There were six further series against New Zealand up to 1914, when WWI intervened. During that period, NSW played New Zealand on all the latter's visits to Australia, and these contests were resumed in 1920.

Tours to and from the northern hemisphere took place as long ago as 1888, when the New Zealand Natives toured Australia and Great Britain, playing a record 107 games. Great Britain visited Australia in 1899, and this was followed by the first All Blacks tour of Great Britain, France and North America in 1905. In 1908/09 an Australian side undertook a 38-match northern tour, winning 32, and, as part of the Australasia team, the Gold Medal at the 1908 London Olympics.

By 1923, therefore, international rugby tours were well-established and popular events, the matches attracting great interest and drawing large crowds, the outcome a matter of national importance. For the players, however, they were by modern standards formidable undertakings, not only through the congested nature of the itineraries, but also the travelling involved (not to mention, of course, the legendary hospitality).

Thus the 1923 New South Wales team (never referred to in the contemporary press as 'Waratahs' or for that matter 'Wallabies', but rather, the 'Cornstalks'), commenced their tour with a 1,400-mile boat-ride across the commonly stormy Tasman in mid-winter. And stormy it proved to be, as the *Post* reported on 14 August that 'the New South Wales Rugby team … will not arrive from Sydney until to-morrow morning, the Manuka having been delayed on the Tasman Sea'.

They were not given long to recover from the voyage before embarking on an itinerary of ten games in 32 days, two a week, including three internationals. They were a young side, most too young to have gone to war, referred to in one cutting as 'colts'. Some 13 of the 24 were under 23 years of age, including an 18- and a 19-year-old. Of the remaining 11, the oldest was 28.

Such a tour demands a warm-up – a pipe-opener – and the team chosen to provide this exercise was not an up-country minnow, if any such minnows existed in those times, but a major provincial team in the form of Wellington. And not simply Wellington, but a combined Wellington-Manawatu team. The basis on which selection was made is not given, but it appears from comparing team sheets that the Manawatu contingent in the starting XV were Galpin locking the scrum and Brophy as wing-three-quarter. While we do not know if the sprinkling of Manawatu players was seen as stiffening or weakening the team, we can be reasonably sure that it was not the intention of the hosts to let the visitors off lightly. In fact, both Manawatu players received favourable mention in the match reports, two of which name the home team simply as 'Wellington', and only one as 'Wellington-Manawatu'.

Wellington-Manawatu v. New South Wales, 18 August 1923

According to the *Dominion*, the teams were as follows:

NEW SOUTH WALES

Loudon
Erasmus, Trousdale, Buntine, Smith
George
Duncan
Elliott, Ferguson, Thorn
Pearce (rep. Blackwood), Armstrong
Thompson, Fowles, Davis

WELLINGTON

Malcolm
Svenson, H.G. Nicholls, Brophy
F. Tilyard, M.F. Nicholls
H.E. Nicholls
Porter (wing forward)
A. Thomas, C.B. Thomas
Galpin, Pringle
Duncan
Swain, Osborne

The line-ups are interesting, and in the case of the forwards, of great relevance. The visitors appear to have been playing inside/outside centres, as opposed to the home team's first and second five-eighths. Wellington played a 2-3-2 scrum with a loose wing forward who fed the ball into the scrum, while NSW were playing an eight-man scrum with a three-man front row in a 3-2-3 combination.

'Tackler' in the NZ *Truth* of 25 August 1923 reported the match as follows:

**BRILLIANT RUGBY
WELLINGTON DEFEAT NSW
SPECTACULAR BACK PLAY**

Played in the presence of over 15,000 spectators, under most ideal weather conditions, the combined Wellington-Manawatu team defeated the New South Wales team at Athletic Park on Saturday by 29 points to 16. The game was productive of much spectacular back play and it was without doubt, the most brilliant display of the code seen in Wellington for some time. With the initial exchanges over the home team jumped into its stride and clapped on the pace. The blacks did not give the visitors a moment to take stock and the suddenness of the Wellington concerted attack unbalanced the Welshmen. The earlier disjointed efforts of the home team, as seen in previous matches, was replaced by machine-like movements that were upsetting the blues defence. Seeing the plight of the opposition, **'Ginger' Nicholls** and his men started out to make hay while the sun was shining. They did, and with a vengeance. With a quarter of an hour gone the home players were eight points up from two brilliant efforts by the rear-guard. Wellington backs and forwards were playing the game as they had never played it before. Their combined work was bringing them tries – all highly spectacular – and at the spell the score was 21 to 3. The pace up to this stage had been a veritable cracker, and it was questionable whether the players could stand up to it in the second half.

Later, 'Tackler' waxed even more lyrical:

> The whole Wellington team on the day was perfect. Each player knew what was expected of him and he carried out his task to the utmost letter. Instead of waiting to see how play was going to proceed the home backs decided to take control and make the play suit their requirements. This bold attitude was highly successful right from the outset, and the policy of 'wait and see' so fondly cherished by the black rear-guard was dropped – and let us hope, for the good.

And he even verged on the poetic:

> From all manner of places the Wellington skipper sent his men away. The combination was perfect, each man sent on his pass at the right time, a cut-in was executed at the psychological moment, and then an opponent was fooled beautifully. With such tactics in operation what could one expect but try upon try? And what was going on in the opposition camp during these concerted attacks! There was confusion in the ranks, all plans of attack were shattered, and defensive work was being carried out in a half-hearted sort of way. It must have been a welcome sound to the tourists when half-time was signalled. The break was wanted badly to repair the damage created by the Wellington assaults.

The *Dominion* of 20 August 1923 saw things a little differently:

> Due to an inglorious display of feeble tackling in the first spell, they [i.e., the visitors] were up against Wellington's lead of 18 points at the commencement of the second half, the Wellington backs having enjoyed the weak defence to the utmost, running, passing, selling the 'dummy', and dodging to their sweet will, and providing an exhilarating exhibition.

Nonetheless, the *Dominion* correspondent noted 'a side can only play as well as the opposition will allow it' and described some great tries. In the first try, '**H.E. Nicholls** set the movement afoot with a smart pass to **Tilyard** who sent the ball on to **Mark Nicholls**, who made a promising opening, and transferred to **"Doc" Nicholls**. The Wellington centre sent out a good pass to **Brophy**, who dashed across with Loudon and Smith at his heels.' In the second try: 'Gathering in a return from Trousdale in home territory, **H.E. Nicholls** eluded a brace of tacklers and passed to **M. Nicholls**, who ran down field, beating man after man, and, when finally tackled, he transferred to **Tilyard,** who had followed up smartly, and who touched down under the posts.'

There comes, however, a brief set-back: 'From the kick-out New South Wales attacked, and in a handy position, the Wellington hookers were penalised for lifting their feet in the scrum. Buntine's kick was a good one, and opened the Blues' scoring account.'

But the *New Zealand Sportsman* of 18 August, perhaps somewhat unsportingly, wrote: 'The Aussies got their first score from a good penalty kick by Buntine, a goal being awarded, although the ball appeared to fall short.'

Back to the *Dominion* for Wellington's third try:

> One of the neatest 'dummies' was responsible for Wellington's next try. **Porter** broke away and sent the ball down the paddock with a well-directed kick. The leather rebounded off Loudon's chest into the arms of the Wellington wing-forward [viz the same **Porter**] but the latter lost possession. **Tilyard**, however, snapped the ball up and passed to **'Doc' Nicholls**, who raced down the line in company with **Svenson**. Everybody believed that the ball was given to **Svenson** when Smith was reached, but in a flash **Nicholls** had ducked under the winger's arms and was over the line to score a beautiful try.

Now the fourth try: '**Malcolm**, the full-back, initiated the bout which resulted in Wellington's next try. The ball was handled in turn by **M. Nicholls, Svenson** and **Tilyard**, the last-named cutting in and scoring under the posts.' (The *New Zealand Sportsman* wrote of **Tilyard** 'beating several players with a clever corkscrew run and scored a great try.')

And the *Dominion* on the fifth try and the last of the half:

> Neatly eluding the opposing pack, **H.E. Nicholls** dispatched the leather to **M. Nicholls**, from whom it was transferred to **Tilyard**, who passed to **'Doc' Nicholls**. The Wellington centre raced down the field and send [sic] the ball on to **Brophy**, who passed in-field to **Tilyard**, to **C.B. Thomas** [a forward!] who scored under the posts. [That move involved the entire back-line, one twice, with the exception of one winger and the full-back!] The visitors had brightened up a little, but they had still failed to enter the picture when the bell rang.

Let us return to 'Tackler', who wrote:

> The second spell opened sensationally. Erasmus fielded the kick-off and at top threaded his way through the defence, only to be brought down a few yards from his objective. The visitors changed their tactics. Up to this juncture they had been content to play a defensive game, but the defence had failed to come up to expectations. Back and forward alike started to throw it about with delightful abandon and ground was gained. A good forward rush saw Ferguson get over, but the Wellington backs retaliated with a fine movement that **'Doc' Nicholls** finished off. It was a lucky try as **Svenson** threw the leather over his head and it landed in **Nicholl's** hands. **Swain** scored next for the home team and **Malcolm**'s kick made the score 29 as against the visitors' 6, but two tries by Thorne [sic], converted by Bunting, brought their total to 16, and that was how the score stood at the no-side bell. ... The pace of the first spell left its mark, and half-way through the second both fifteens started to let up. The Wellington team were guilty of this more than the visitors, and Thorn's first try was a gift. He was unmarked in the line-out, the ball was tipped to him, and he only had to fall over.

The *Dominion* noted that Thorn's second try 'was the outcome of the fine work of George, who had been the heart and soul of his team'.

One more incident from the play is worth mentioning. With the score at 11-3, '[t]he blacks were having the all best [sic] of things and **Pringle** was nearly over, **A. Thomas** knocking on his pass out' (*New Zealand Sportsman*, 18 August 1923). And from the *NZ Truth* of 25 August 1923: 'Pringle, the elongated Wellington player, was the best forward on the ground in the NSW match. In previous matches "Nugget" has been most noticeable in line-out play, ... using his reach to advantage, but on Saturday last he was always in the thick of the fray. He would have scored in the first spell had he gone on himself instead of passing to Thomas.'

The other journalists concurred regarding Nugget's display. 'Tackler' felt: 'Without doubt Pringle was the best forward on the paddock. He used his reach to some order, but in loose or tight work he was equally at home. His display was his best to date.' According to the *Dominion*: 'Among the forwards Pringle took the eye for consistent good work.' And the *New Zealand Sportsman* of 25 August reported: 'In the forwards, Pringle stood out head and shoulders above any other player.'

Wellington v. New South Wales: Analysis

Another way of phrasing the old adage is that you can only play the opposition you are given, and it does not detract from Wellington's superlative display, particularly in the first half, to admit that the NSW team was under-cooked and ill-prepared for this encounter. 'Tackler' opined that:

> It would not be proper to condemn the New South Welshmen on the day's play as being a poor combination. They fielded a team far below their best and the majority of the players were unknown to each other, in the sense that they had never had a game together before. ... Then again, several of the participants had not recovered from their rough sea voyage and could not display anything like their best form.

The *Dominion* correspondent wrote: 'When the team left Sydney, the critics were of the opinion that never before was New South Wales so weak in half-backs. Perhaps it is hardly fair to judge their prospects on Saturday's game as six of their best men are not yet with them. ... The six newcomers may bring the missing qualities, in which case the team will do well later on.' In this context, it is noteworthy that only three of the backs and four of the forwards (including Blackwood) who appeared in this match were in the starting XV for the Second Test.

The explanation for the team's unfamiliarity and the missing six was provided by the *Post* on 15 August: 'About eleven players had been unable to get away.' Jobs were hard to come by at the time, with unavailability causing selectors problems for touring teams both national and international. 'Tackler' discussed this at some length in relation to Wellington, advocating that the Football Union liaise with the employers. And as for the missing six, they were 'Varsity students having remained behind in Sydney to sit for examinations' and would arrive in time for the Dunedin test. In all, ten of the 27 had visited New Zealand before with Varsity or NSW teams.

Of greater interest, however, particularly from the point of view of tactics, is the forward battle: 3-2-3 or 2-3-2? The *Dominion* thought well of the NSW forwards '[which] are at present their ray of hope. Strong and vigorous and fast, they have developed the Springbok style of tight packing [it was they who developed the 3-4-1 scrum] and the snappy short pass in the loose, the latter being very dangerous to their opponents.' New Zealand had always played a 2-3-2 scrum – commonly attributed to the 1905 team but in fact first toyed with by the New Zealand Natives in their northern tour in 1888/89 – and the Australians were very familiar with it. 'Tackler' wrote:

> The NSW 3-2-3 scrum was the equal of the Wellington 2-3-2 formation when it came to hooking, and the visitors gave their half more than a fair share of the ball [when NSW would have had a weight advantage]. In loose scrummages the black players always held the advantage, but the balance of weight was with Wellington and this accounted for a lot of the home team's success in this department.

However, in the first half, it was the wing forward who caused the problems, as he was able, with the ball being the off-side line, to be among the opposing inside backs as soon as the ball left the scrum. Not only that, but on a home heel, he stood in the way of the on-rushing defence – indeed, a whinging Aussie journalist was quoted in the *Evening Post* the previous year complaining that as soon as the ball was heeled he was automatically off-side. A matter for the referee, of course! According to the *Dominion*: 'A thorn in the side of the visitors was the wing-forward, and it was quite clear early in the game that they are not used to this harassing individual at home, and in the second half they took one of their men out of the scrum to play opposite Porter.' And this from 'Tackler': 'Porter was on his game and during the first spell he was repeatedly in the picture. Of course, he had no opposition, but in the second half he did not come into prominence so much. Elliott saw to that [having been] taken out of the scrum to counter the marauding tendencies of Porter.' The *Dominion* reached a similar conclusion but added, interestingly and perhaps not surprisingly:

> Porter had his own way in the first half, and he was fortunate that some of his off-side play went unnoticed. ... The referee was far too tolerant to breaches of the rules in the scrummages, and to an extent these forward tussles spoilt the game. Obstruction was also very rife and the greater part of it went unchecked, until the players began to come to grips in real earnest, when warnings had to be issued by the referee.

The *New Zealand Sportsman* noted that in the first half 'a little spar between Davis and Porter by the side of the scrum amused the crowd' and concluded that 'one very pleasing feature about [Porter's] play ... was that he kept a cool head when he was receiving unnecessary attention from one of the NSW players.' In the end, 'Tackler' contented himself with: 'It was not an easy game to referee, and Referee Simpson had a hard task, but he came through the ordeal well.'

It is interesting to note that, with their differing scrum formations, the All Blacks and Springboks fought out two close drawn series in that decade, home and away, although in the 1928 tour of South Africa the All Blacks put a third man in the front row for their own feeds. The issue was resolved ultimately in 1932 when the 2-3-2 scrum was outlawed.

From Wellington, the New South Welshmen travelled south, defeating South Canterbury 23-16 in Timaru midweek, while on their way to Dunedin for the first test.

New South Wales v. New Zealand, Saturday, 25 August 1923, Dunedin, The First Test: A Tad Unlucky for Pringle

Two telegrams, handwritten in pencil, recognise Nugget's late withdrawal. They are set out below:[4]

Telegram date-stamped Dunedin, NZ, 24 August 1923
3/40 p Courtenay Place [Wellington]
Pringle & Tilyard
NZ Football Team
Dunedin

Plenty ginger repeat Saturday's
form good luck
Wallace

Telegram date-stamped Dunedin, NZ, 25 August 1923
10/18a Wellington
12
Nugget Pringle
All Blacks
Dunedin

Stiff luck all ranks
regret indisposition
Brown

---

4 Doubtless, Wallace is Billy Wallace. Tilyard was the other Wellington player.

NZ Truth gives the reason for Nugget's non-appearance: 'Both Bell and Pringle, who stood down on Saturday through injuries, the former with ulcers on his leg and the latter with a "cauliflower ear"[5] are hopeful of lining out at Lancaster Park. *"Nugget" proved a great entertainer at Brighton, and his Salome dance was a scream'* [emphasis added]. Nugget can be seen to have a swollen right ear in the team and individual photographs prior to the First Test. In fact, in the course of 1923, he had one ear lanced *five* times and the other *seven*, for the condition.[6] In the team and action photographs of the Second Test it comes as no surprise to see that he is wearing headgear. As for a 6'5" Salome, the mind boggles. While he did not make a physical contribution to the match itself, Nugget must have had a very positive impact on team spirit. Big veils indeed!

And they were needed! 'Tackler' wrote in the *NZ Truth* of 1 September 1923 that arrangements for the training camp were

---

5   The external ear or pinna, on which spectacles rest, is made of elastic fibrocartilage, overlain by a thin external lining, the perichondrium, from which its blood supply is derived. The skin of the ear is closely stuck to the perichondrium without fatty tissue in-between. As a result of direct blows or shearing forces (commonly in boxing, wrestling and rugby), the skin and perichondrium are torn away from the cartilage. This causes bleeding, which accumulates between the cartilage and its lining. If the pressure is not released and the blood supply restored, the cartilage dies and crumbles, healing by scarring in a misshapen fashion, supposedly giving the ear the appearance of a cauliflower. Treatment now and 100 years ago is and was the same: the urgent release of the collection of blood by lancing, or these days, sometimes drawn off by needle and syringe. By the look of Nugget's ear in later photographs, it wasn't always done quickly enough in his case!

6   According to 'Racket' ('Rapid Rise in Rugby', June 1939), and to family legend.

> far from satisfactory … the necessary arrangements for the billeting of the twenty selected players was left to the Otago Union, and that body decided on the seaside resort, Brighton. The team assembled at Dunedin late on the night of the 21st and were taken by 'bus part of the way. The last 2 miles had to be walked, and the quarters were reached just on midnight, where the team had its first solid meal after leaving Oamaru at 6 p.m. But that was not so bad. Then arose the trouble of how to provide the necessary sleeping accommodation for the party. The boarding house was not big enough, and so three and four men were put in a room. … The climax was reached next morning when the team went out to train. The ground that was expected to serve the purpose was partially under water, and as there was no other alternative the practices were carried out on the road. The day before the game sufficient water had cleared from the 'ground' and so a spin was held on it, but not for too long. Throughout the practice the players had to keep one eye on the game and one eye on the ground. … Then, to cap the lot, the team arrived at the ground about a quarter of an hour before the game was due to commence, and in that short space of time the trainer was expected to give the fifteen chosen a good rub down.

The Union would certainly have wanted to draw Salome's veils over that one, although, if 15 angry men wanted to take it out on someone, who better than 15 Australians?! For the record, New Zealand won the match 19–9.

NSW now travelled further south to Invercargill, where on 29 August they were trounced 31-9 by Southland, before heading north again for the second test at Lancaster Park.

BACK IN "CAMP" – Timaru Turns It On

From the *Timaru Herald*, Monday 27th August 1923: The selectors had 'made some drastic changes [...] (D)ropped' were Steel, Snodgrass, Tilyard, Mill, Gemmell, Righton and Mackereth, replaced by Ford, Lucas, Perry, H.E. Nicholls, McLean, West and Irvine. The chosen 20 were to 'meet at Timaru to prepare for the second test'.

Ibid, 28th August: Those who 'retained their places' had arrived by the express the previous afternoon. 'The northern players who lost their places were also through passengers on the same train.' Oops! The players were 'quartered at the Grosvenor', and later 'had a run at the Caledonian Grounds'. That afternoon they were to be 'guests of the S.C.R.U. at the Schools tourney, and to-night they will attend the boxing match [...] Tomorrow they will be taken to see the Wairarapa game at Temuka. For Thursday a motor trip in the country is projected, and probably a musical evening will follow.' And indeed it did.

Ibid, 30th August: The team had been 'training steadily', with 'early morning exercise on Caroline Bay and a practice later'. They were well pleased with the weather and other conditions and expected to take the field 'in much better shape than [...] in Dunedin'. They had watched athletics events and 'this afternoon a cricket match has been arranged'. Nugget must have enjoyed that.

Ibid, Saturday 1st September: The team left by train for Christchurch the previous afternoon, given a 'hearty send-off' by a large crowd. Before leaving the Grosvenor, Mr A.J.Griffiths presented Mr H.H.Fraser, S.C.R.U. president, with 'a gold pencil case, suitably inscribed', in thanks for the Union's officials' endeavours on behalf of the players.

V WARATAHS, FIRST TEST, 1923

Fig.14. Caricature, originally published in N.Z. Truth, 4 August 1923. Note the shin-pads.

Fig.15. In training camp before the first test, 1923. See p.53.

Fig.16. A cauliflower ear.

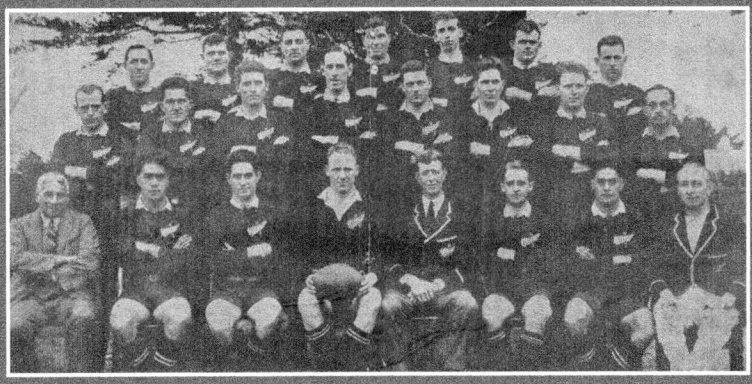

Fig.17. All Black first test team, training camp, Brighton, 1923. "Back row:- J.R.Bell, J.Steel, D.McMeeking, F.A.Bellis, F.J.Tilyard, L.Righton, W.F.Snodgrass. Middle – Q.Donald, S.Gemmell, M.J.Brownlie, A.Pringle, R.G.B Sinclair, L.C.Petersen, A.L.Williams, J.Mackereth. Front – W.Parata (selector), W.P.Potaka, J.Mill, J.Richardson, A.J.Griffiths (manager), P.F.McCarthy, P. Peina (mistakenly captioned P.Potaka), A.Mercer (trainer)." (Identified with help from Ron Palenski.)

NEW ZEALAND POST OFFICE TELEGRAPHS.

Recd. at
From
By
Ackd. by

Note.—This form must accompany any inquiry made respecting this telegram.

Sent at
To
By
Ackgt. recd. by

Checked by
741

Office Stamp
TELEGRAPH OFFICE 24 AUG 23 DUNEDIN N.Z.

Courtenay Place 16
Pringle & Tilyard
NZ Footballs Team Dunedin
Plenty ginger repeat saturdays form good luck
Wallace

Figs.18 & 19. Good luck and hard luck telegrams.

NEW ZEALAND POST OFFICE TELEGRAPHS.

Recd. at
From
By
Ackd. by

Note.—This form must accompany any inquiry made respecting this telegram.

Sent at
To
By
Ackgt. recd. by

Checked by
266

Office Stamp
TELEGRAPH OFFICE 25 AUG 23 DUNEDIN N.Z.

Wellington 12
nugget Pringle all Blacks Dunedin
Stiff luck's all hands regret indisposition

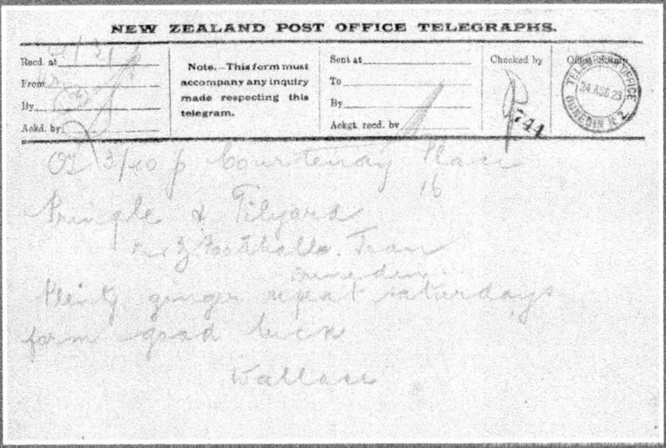

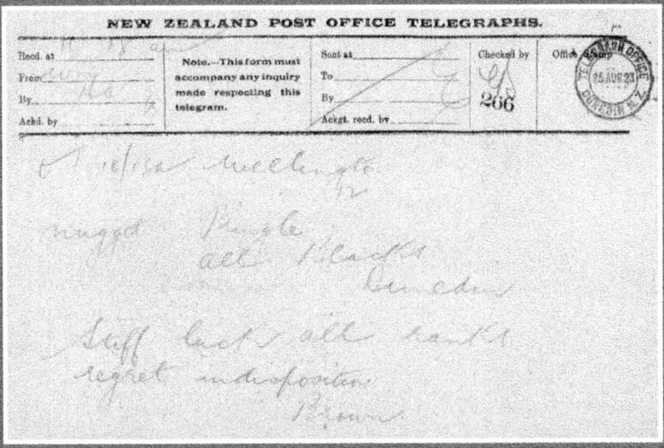

CHAPTER 6

The Second Test

**NEW SOUTH WALES V. NEW ZEALAND,
Saturday, 1 September 1923,
Lancaster Park, Christchurch**

Nugget set a record: 'Pringle (Wellington) has the distinction of being the tallest player ever seen on Lancaster Park [says the *Christchurch Star*]. His height is 6 feet 4 inches.' He received, this time, personal good luck telegrams from Brown (and 'all club members'), Jack Prew, 'Fred', 'Duncan' and Arthur Thomas. The last two may have been his fellow Wellington reps. Courtesy of the scrapbook, we have the benefit of comprehensive match reports in the *New Zealand Sportsman*, the *Times*, the *Dominion* and the *Evening Post*, together with an analysis by Tackler in *NZ Truth*. First, this from the *Evening Post* of 3 September 1923:

'Every player is right out to get the Ashes,' remarked Mr A.J. Griffiths, manager of the New Zealand team, in speaking to a *Post* reporter prior to the match. 'Every player realises the responsibility which rests upon his shoulders in the effort to regain the Ashes, and thereby bring back the prestige of New Zealand football. If we are beaten to-day we will accept it in the right spirit, and we will be the first to congratulate the winners – and good luck to them! Defeat to-day will mean that we will have to go harder, if that is possible, to win the third Test, but I don't think any team could go harder than our players to-day. They have had five hours' football every day while at Timaru. We have no complaints this week, though I would have liked to have Lucas a bit earlier. The training programme each day included physical drill, talk on tactics, forward and back work, etc. The players were out on training work from 7.15 a.m. to 12.30 or 1 p.m. … If we win,' Mr Griffiths added, 'well, in all probability new players will be given a chance in the third Test. That is our intention in view of the big tour next year.'

The *Times* reported:

> Before leaving for the ground the New Zealand team assembled to express its appreciation of the abilities of Mr A.J. Griffiths as manager and coach of the team. J. Richardson, the captain, on behalf of the team, handed to Mr Griffiths a leather dressing case, suitably inscribed. It was always team first and last with Mr Griffiths, said the captain, and members of the team felt that they could not let the occasion pass, as there might be changes in the team for the third test [as indeed there were!], without showing appreciation of the manager's efforts in Brighton and Timaru. Any little situations that cropped up were handled with tact by Mr Griffiths, who had set a standard which other managers would find hard to follow. The New Zealand Rugby Union would have no cause to worry about the conduct of teams with men like Mr Griffiths in charge of the players. In reply Mr Griffiths stated that anything he had done had been for the good of the game. He had endeavoured to do his best for the players, and if they won that would be ample compensation. He felt that Nelson's message at Trafalgar might be suitably applied to the present occasion: 'New Zealand expects every man this day will do his duty.' Mr Griffiths thanked the players for their gift.

The *Evening Post* once more:

> **RUGBY HONOURS**
> **THE 'ASHES' REGAINED**
> **ALL BLACKS SCORE HEAVILY**
> **SECOND TEST AT CHRISTCHURCH**
> **NEW SOUTH WELSHMEN SUFFER THEIR BIGGEST DEFEAT**
>
> The second act of this year's most important Rugby drama was staged at Lancaster Park on Saturday afternoon, the chosen representatives of New South Wales and New Zealand engaging in another struggle for the 'Ashes', which were in possession of the visitors. New Zealand's claim to superiority over the State which has kept the amateur game going against great odds, and which is now entering upon better days, was advanced in a most convincing manner, with the result that the visitors sustained the greatest defeat which has been encountered by any Australian or New South Wales team in Rugby Tests in New Zealand. The All Blacks won by 34 points to 6.

The win to New Zealand was not unexpected, but the margin of 28 points was surprising. While that perhaps does not represent the difference between the teams on the day's play, it bears striking testimony to the value of making serious preparation for important events. The New Zealand representatives benefited considerably from a period of several days training at Timaru. The prestige of New Zealand on the Rugby field was at stake, and it was their business to demonstrate that all was well with New Zealand's national game. Prior to taking the field on Saturday, the All Blacks received a final message from their guardian (Mr A.J. Griffiths). It was this: 'New Zealand expects that every man this day will do his duty.' Spurred on by that, the All Blacks achieved a notable success, in which a fine pack of forwards, with a great wing, E.A. Bellis, carried off the honours.

The weather was ideal, and the ground was hard, much harder than the New Zealand players have been accustomed to this season. Some of the contestants received injuries during the game, though there was no rough play. Bellis, Ford and Petersen, of the All Black team, were compelled to retire, the first-named having a shoulder dislocated.

Encircling the playing area on Saturday afternoon there were many rows of people closely packed, those in front on seats, and those on the small slopes and higher ground standing shoulder to shoulder, the whole, including three crowded stands, making up a crowd of nearly 14,000 which is not a great deal short of the record attendance for the ground. ... Christchurch, for some days previously, had been experiencing north-west weather, and in consequence the ground had been hardened. During Saturday morning, however, a south-west wind made the outlook unpromising, the more when it brought rain showers. Better skies heartened those who were off to the match early in the afternoon, and for the game the weather was almost perfect, the south-west wind dropping to practically a calm during the progress of play. The morning's rain showers had not softened the ground. South Island primary school teams, Otago and South Canterbury, fighting the tournament final, kept the spectators interested for an hour or so before the big event. Those boys played good football, and some were quite good enough to be termed pocket editions of the players engaged in the greater test to follow. Items from the Christchurch Tramways Band were also entertaining.

> An eager crowd waiting for the appearance of the honoured players of the two Rugby countries, New Zealand, the greater of the two, became very enthusiastic as the big Southlander, 'Jock' Richardson, headed the procession of All Blacks. Immediately behind him came **Williams, Pringle, Bellis, West** and **Petersen**, then the file tailed off till **Peina** and the tiny **McCarthy** brought up the rear, ... W.J.B. Sheehan followed in the lead of the file of sky-blue jerseys. Both captains carried mascots. Taking up position in line on the field each team gave its prelude to the notable event, the All Blacks supplying a haka, and the New South Welshmen a war-cry,[1] following which the band played the National Anthem to add to the pomp and ceremony of the occasion.

---

1 According to Tackler (*NZ Truth*, 1 September 1923): 'Not many at the NSW-Wellington match could make anything out of the Cornstalks' war-cry. Here it is:
   Gau, Gau, New Zealand, Wir-r-r?
   Mu-i-an yil-ling
   Bu rang ul lan yang
   Yai, yai, Gun-yil-lan-yang,
   YAP!
   The *New Zealand Sun* of 31 August 1923 confirmed these lines, give or take minor transpositions, and carried a picture of 'the All Blacks [who] will have something to counter this'. The *Sun* photographer has caught the All Blacks, heavily disguised in white jerseys, practising a war dance, as they chant 'Harihari, harihari'. The translation of this is 'We will pull together', which is what they appear to be doing, each man bending and pulling on the flexed right leg of the man in front! The scrapbook also carries a picture of the 'New South Welshmen completing their war-cry' – in a line, with one man facing the same way in front, arms upstretched, leaping up (one would have thought – although their feet are still on the ground!).

The teams shaped up as follows:

NEW SOUTH WALES

O.E. Nothling, 13st 5lb

D.J. Erasmus, 13st 4lb; R. Loudon, 13st 6lb; W.B.J. Sheehan, 10st 7lb (captain); R.G. Stanley, 10st 12lb

W.G. George, 10st 6lb

N. Mingay, 10st 0lb

R. Elliott, 12st 8lb

A.R. Armstrong, 13st; E.J. Thorn, 13st 7lb; H.C. Taylor, 13st; W.J. Marrott, 13st; T.S.R. Davis, 12st 7lb

J.G. Blackwood, 12st; A.B. Erby, 12st 10lb

NEW ZEALAND

R.G.B. Sinclair, 12st 7lb

W.A. Ford, 10st 7lb; F. Lucas, 11st 8lb; Peina, 10st 7lb

F. Perry, 11st 3lb; R. Bell, 12st 6lb

P. McCarthy, 10st 5 lb

E.A. Bellis*, 13st 12lb

A. Pringle, 13st 12lb; J. Richardson, 14st 7lb (captain); L. Petersen, 13st 6lb; L. Williams, 14st 9lb; A. West, 13st 9lb

D. McMeeking, 12st 6lb; Q. Donald, 13st 3lb

*(sic) The contemporary press commonly misspelt Moke Belliss's surname thus.

From the *New Zealand Times* of 3 September 1923 comes the following match report:

A GAME STRUGGLE

The first spell of the encounter will go down in history as one of the gamest exhibitions on the part of a light forward team ever seen in the Dominion. Right from the beginning the sheer weight of the All Black forwards battered big gaps in the Australian ranks. Locked in the scrums the Dominion pack proved immovable, and all the efforts of the Kangaroos early 3-2-3 pack and their later 3-4 formation could not gain an inch. But almost from the beginning the All Black hookers were beaten. The first few scrums saw honours even, later the Australians showed themselves definitely superior, and Mingay, nimblest of half-backs, had plenty of chances. Many times the scrum went down badly or screwed, and with increasing frequency in the second spell manoeuvring was necessary before they approached the spot where the scrum had been ordered.

THE PRICE OF POSSESSION

The Australian hookers were penalised often enough, but it was a cheap price to pay for possession of the ball as frequently as they got it. ... By far the majority of the scrums saw the blue backs go away, and with a little more steadiness in attack some of these movements, dangerous enough in all conscience, would have resulted in tries. At a conservative estimate from 65 to 70% of the scrums were won by the men from over the water.

SCRUMS AND STOPPAGES

The scrum work became so important because the match was a game of scrums and stoppages. The incessant packing was one factor in wearing down eight Kangaroo forwards who were nevertheless finely trained and fit. The large number of breaks due to injuries to players (mainly blacks) who seemed determined to take their full three minutes grace, was a factor which aided the Australians particularly in the opening spell. The number of stoppages in the first spell was extraordinary, and at one time the players were going down like ninepins. Two and three men needed attention together, **Bellis** and **Q. Donald** being down at one moment, **Ford**, Davis and Nothling at another. ... **Richardson** also seemed out for a period, then skipped up like an antelope, much to the amusement of the crowd.

MAGNIFICENT FORWARDS

Right from the beginning of the match it was evident that the pace of the New Zealand forwards would brew trouble for the best defence. They rucked like one man, they gained in mastery in the lineout, the Kangaroos striving solely to give their backs possession, and not trying to take the ball forward. Though securing in the scrum, the blue pack could not serve their rearguard as often as they should have done, first because of the agility of **Bellis**, who was not to blame when the ball was whipped out; secondly because of the swiftness with which the black pack broke up to the command as soon as their hookers were beaten and resolved the scrum into a battle of the loose. [T]he All Black tackling was deadly, and the forwards assisted in defence tremendously. … [E]ach of these failures by the visiting rearguard saw the beginning of a dangerous New Zealand forward rush. One of the most magnificent packs which ever went on the field to represent the Dominion hammered its way through the weak Australian centre with growing ease, and although the home back-line alos [sic – should this be 'also' or 'alas'?– or both!] failed to justify itself, the terrific rushes by the massive black forwards battered openings in the Australian ranks.

The telegraphed match report from *New Zealand Sportsman* of 1 September 1923 gives details of the run of play:

> Kicking off, NZ played with the sun at their backs but with a slight breeze in opposition. Play landed in the Welshmen's 25 [long before the dreaded metrication!] and for off-side play by NSW, NZ were awarded a free kick, **Sinclair** failing. The game was taken to NZ territory, where **McCarthy** relieved with a mark. Much high kicking resulted [*plus ça change!*] until NZ organised a passing rush, which **Bell** spoilt by a knock on. Play was drifting up and down field, and **Sinclair** neatly stopped a forward rush by NSW. An infringement by the visitors gave NZ a scrum in NSW's 25, from which the ball travelled from **Petersen** to **Bellis**, to **Donald**, who scored a sensational try near the posts. **Sinclair** made no mistake in converting.
>
> New Zealand ... 5
New South Wales ... 0

The visitors immediately attacked and Erasmus secured and passed to Elliott, who was forced out. Owing to **Bellis** getting hurt, play was stopped for a few minutes until he was able to go on. A NSW attack was repelled, and from a scrum in mid-field, NZ backs were set in motion and passed down field, but **Ford** failed to take Lucas' pass which was low. From a tussle NZ had the advantage of being awarded a free kick which **Sinclair** failed to goal. [At this point, the *Dominion* reported, without further elaboration or explanation: 'The referee had been putting the ball into the scrummage, but now entrusted that task to the players.'] A penalty kick was taken for the Welshmen by Nothling, whose kick landed perilously near NZ's goal. Another score was fast coming New Zealand's way when **Williams** in the van, fell over the line from a melee and scored the All Blacks' second try. **Sinclair**'s shot proved inaccurate.

New Zealand ... 8
New South Wales ... 0

Next, the report goes on to describe how Pringle scores:

> Great excitement now prevailed when the leather was whipped out from **Bell** to **Lucas**, to **Ford**, the last-named being grassed by an excellent tackle by Nothling right at the corner. Play now ceased while Nothling was having an injured hand attended to. When he went on again, the game resumed in the Blues' 25. A forward rush saw **Pringle** score at the corner with **Bellis** and others in attendance. **Sinclair** succeeded in landing between the posts, – the best kick of the day.
>
> New Zealand ... 13
New South Wales ... 0

In the words of the *Times*: 'The ball came (**Ford's**) way and he sent in a low pass, which struck a blue forward and bounced back. The black pack carried it along, **Pringle** ultimately snapping it up and touching down.' While the *Dominion* reported: 'Shortly after, with play on the other side of the field, it was thought the ball had gone into touch, but **Pringle**, following it closely, snapped it up, and scored.'

And we now resume the *Sportsman*'s match report:

Offside play gave NSW a penalty kick, but Nothling made a wretched attempt. Play was confined to the neutral zone until a long kick up-field by the Aussies was returned immediately. After vigorous play amongst the vanguard in the vicinity of the Blues' 25, Stanley took a neat mark and punted far up-field, but the leather was returned by the heavy NZ forwards. An incident which caused excitement in the first spell was when the Aussies were awarded an obstructional free kick for which **Sinclair** was responsible. The kick took play to half-way. ...

On resuming [after half-time], the All Blacks had the disadvantage of the sun, but nevertheless they made the pace. **Brownlie** [i.e., M. Brownlie] replaced **Petersen**, who was injured during the latter stage of the first spell, and **Ford** was replaced by **Potaka**. A fast rush by NSW backs eventuated in Elliott taking a mark in NZ's 25. It was a bad attempt. Shortly afterwards, New South Wales account was opened by a good passing rush from the half-back to the wing, Erasmus, who ran over the line and scored in fine style. Mingay failed to convert.

New Zealand ... 13
New South Wales ... 3

Instantly the ball was taken down at the Blacks' toes, and the Welshmen had many a trying situation[2] until the effort was capped by **Lucas** securing a good score as the result of a great dash. **Sinclair** failed.

> New Zealand ... 16
> New South Wales ... 3

Bellis now took possession and dashed upfield, Nothling saving with a good tackle. New Zealand's score was now increased by a free kick by **Sinclair**.

> New Zealand ... 19
> New South Wales ... 3

Again the Blacks were offensive [in the nicest possible way, one hopes] and a passing rush initiated by **McCarthy** went on to **Lucas**, who passed forward and spoiled an almost certain score.

---

2   This included: 'An interception and a dash by **Bellis** added to the liveliness of the proceedings, and there was a sigh of relief from the New South Wales supporters when a force-down saved **Pringle** from scoring, after **Brownlie** had made an effort' (*Evening Post*, 3 September 1923).

The *Dominion* takes up the story here:

> Nine points were scored in as many minutes, and the pace of the game gradually increased until the spectators were roaring with excitement. The tumult soon died down, however, as the All Black forwards, taking advantage of loose handling of the ball by their backs [sic] took complete control of the game, and commenced piling on the points. **Brownlie, Pringle, Bellis** and **Richardson** took part in a rush that would have broken any defence had it been supported by the backs; a pass forward by **Potaka** lost another try. **Perry**, who was the star of an indifferent back-line, set **McMeeking** across the line, but play was recalled for a knock-on.

Now back to the *Sportsman*:

> At half-way, **Sinclair** took a penalty kick for NZ, but he was not successful, the leather striking one of the posts. A speculator by Nothling was taken by **Lucas** who knocked on. The consequent scrum saw the NSW backs rushing down the field, only to be repelled by the New Zealand rearguard. On they came again, and from a scramble Davis and Marrott both fell on the ball together and scored. No conversion.
>
> New Zealand ... 19
New South Wales ... 6

Sinclair cleared a dangerous position on the NZ goal-line, and brought play to half-way. A forward rush in which **Richardson**, **Bellis** and **McMeeking** were prominent was forced down by a Welsh player at the opportune moment. The All Blacks were not to be denied the try, and again a vanguard rush was organised by **Perry** and **Bellis**, who passed to **Richardson**, who touched down under the posts. **Sinclair** converted with ease.

New Zealand ... 24
New South Wales ... 6

At midfield Mingay took the ball from the ruck and passed to Loudon, who was dragged down by **Richardson** and **Peina** in the nick of time. The home backs were set in motion and the ball was thrown to **Peina**, whose speed was not great enough to carry him through. A following forward rush saw **Brownlie** dash over and **Sinclair** converted.

New Zealand ... 29
New South Wales ... 6

> The next score came straight away, when **Bellis,** making an opening run upfield, passed to **Lucas**, who crossed. **Sinclair** converted.³
>
> New Zealand ... 34
New South Wales ... 6
>
> **Bellis** was at this stage taken off injured. Up and down play followed and the bell sounded with the ball in midfield.

The final score was NZ 34, NSW 6.

---

3   All credit to Bellis and Sinclair – it was a bit better than that. According to the *Dominion*, '**Bellis** made a solo dash down the field, fending, and shaking off tacklers in quick succession before passing to **Lucas**, who was grounded by Nothling's tackle, after he had crossed the line and planted the ball. **Sinclair** goaled from the touch-line, and the spectators shouted their applause at his magnificent goal-kicking performance.'

After the Match

> The comment of Mr Bosward, manager of the New South Wales team, on the result was 'we were well stouched'.[4] The teams were entertained to dinner at the United Services Hotel where a number of New Zealand Rugby officials were also present. ... Mr S.F. Wilson, president of the New Zealand Rugby Union, said he was disappointed with the New South Wales team. He felt they had not given as good a showing as they could have at the top of their form. Mr Bosward said: – 'we have no squeal coming. We were beaten on our merits.' He remarked that so long as the New Zealanders were led by men like Richardson and Bellis the good feeling which existed between New South Wales and New Zealand players would continue. (Applause) ('Tackler', *NZ Truth*, 1 September 1923)

But then there were the oysters! Mr Wilson's comments seem surprisingly unfair, as the general consensus was that the Welshmen, particularly the forwards, – although Mingay and Erasmus were also given special mention – had given a good account of themselves. However elsewhere in the *Times* one reads why they might have been a bit off form:

---

4 'Stouch' (or 'stoush') is not to be found in the *Oxford English Dictionary* (OED), but it is in the *Oxford Dictionary of New Zealand English* (ODNZE) as a noun, defined as 'physical violence, especially on the Rugby field', first quoted in 1905: 'to deal out the stoush'. After WWII it also came to mean a battle.

> Mostly the conditions favoured New Zealand, especially in that freshly rested men went on the field. The Australians had been travelling, having oysters and other surprises in Southland, and southern hospitality. Still they pushed, played and fought within the laws of the game men who were actually a stone heavier in the forwards.

And there was more travelling to be done:

> The New South Wales team and officials and the northern members of the New Zealand team left Christchurch by special train at 7.40 o'clock and returned to Wellington by the [overnight] ferry steamer *Wahine* yesterday morning. To-day the New South Wales team leaves for Napier by the 9 o'clock express and will pit its strength against the Ranfurly Shield holders on Wednesday. (*New Zealand Times*, 3 September 1923)

More trouble – and hospitality – in store!

The Referee

The game had been a difficult one to handle and comments on and by the referee are interesting – and somewhat contrasting. 'Mr J.F Peake of Christchurch handled the game satisfactorily, using his whistle with discretion' (*Evening Post*, 3 September 1923).

> Mr J.F. Peake, the referee, in an interview, said he did not think much of the match, judging it from the All Black standard. It was the hardest game to control he had ever experienced. The scrums were frequently badly formed, and there was a good deal of off-side play in the line-out. There was also too much inclination to appeal, and decisions frequently were taken badly. (*New Zealand Times*, 2 September 1923)

And later in the same edition, in an article entitled 'The Test Reviewed':

> The frequency of minor injuries and the constant stoppage of the play, most often exceeding the specified allowance of time, and the mode of replacement of injured players is one urgently needing alteration and correction. Good players invariably learn to play without going off. This is a Rugby truism. Many injured players, like myself, have continued through a game with broken ribs or jaw. There is urgent need for referees to check these nondescript wrangling melees. Mr Peake handled a very difficult proposition well, but with more than his usual allowance of mistakes. Two open cases of double-handed pushing by Thorn and Bellis deserved severe admonition. Opponents not in possession were sent reeling to the ground.

According to the *Dominion*:

> Mr J.F. Peake, who refereed the famous match between the Springboks and the Maoris in Napier, gave general satisfaction with the whistle, although there was comment in the crowd that, in his interpretation of the off-side rule, his decisions favoured New Zealand. No glaring instances were, however, evident from the front seat of the grandstand.

And back to the *Times* again:

> **THE TEST REVIEWED**
> **NZ BACKS DISAPPOINTING**
> **FORWARDS WORLDBEATERS**

From the New Zealand observer's point of view the only good thing about the game apart from the outcome was the forward battle, with 'all kudos' going to the All Blacks. However, of the visitors, the *Times* thought:

> Their plucky play deserves better recognition. In holding their opposition, over a stone per man heavier, the forwards achieved that which is considered an impossibility in the boxing world, except by freaks like Jimmy Wilde.

> Elliott's placement of the ball in the scrummages was an object lesson in correct tactics, whilst Belliss was permitted to bounce it. The erring methods of this player were more than counterbalanced by the Aussies' mode of 'winging it'.[5] The difference between the two packs in tactics was that whereas the Aussies sought all for the open, heeling, back passing, and feeding, the All Blacks strove by close formation, 'steam roller' methods, to overwhelm the opposition. The result was a poor game, from the spectacular [sic] point of view. The constant marking by the Blacks, even when leading by double figures, shows the state of some portions of the play.

---

5   The meaning of 'winging it' is anybody's guess. Presumably, simply 'they improvised'. Dr Ron Palenski, personal communication.

And What of Pringle's Performance?

> **IRRESISTIBLE FORWARDS**
>
> For seventy of the ninety minutes of the game New Zealand was attacking, and for ninety per cent of that time the attack was in the hands of the forwards ... the names of Bellis, Richardson, Brownlie and Pringle may, without any exaggeration of flight or fancy, be mentioned in the same company as Gallaher, Seeling, Tyler and Fanning. Seven tries were scored by New Zealand. Five of those were scored by forwards, and each of the other two was practically a gift from the forwards to the backs who actually grounded the ball. ... 'Thank God New Zealand has forwards in plenty' was a frequent comment by critics after the game, when the prospect of next year's tour of the United Kingdom was being discussed. But where are the backs coming from? On Saturday's evidence they are not yet in sight. (*Dominion*, 3 September 1923)

And from the *Evening Post* of 8 September 1923:

> For the most part they worked unitedly, Richardson, Pringle, Petersen, West, Williams, McMeeking and Q. Donald, with M. Brownlie in place of Petersen in the second spell, all taking a hand in the inspiring display. ... Wellington's sole representative, A. Pringle was given the distinction of being the tallest man who had ever played on the ground. In line-out and loose work he was always good.

And this from 'Tackler' (*NZ Truth*, 8 September 1923):

> Wellington's only rep. in the second test was Pringle, and he was responsible for a fine game. His height is, of course, a great advantage to him, but his usefulness did not end there. In his last few games the work that Pringle has been putting in in the tight has been more noticeable than hitherto and last Saturday he was always in the picture in this branch of the game. He has yet a bit to learn about dribbling, and though he scored a try from a dribble, he on another occasion lost a sure one by booting too hard when only a few feet off the line.

And, finally, these two quotes from the *New Zealand Times*:

> Richardson, Petersen, till he retired, and Williams were giants indeed: three of the finest forwards the Dominion has ever produced, and Pringle, in the best of company, was a worthy team-mate. The Wellington man justified his inclusion to the hilt, and was conspicuous in line-out work and loose. (*New Zealand Times*, 3 September 1923)
>
> Pringle, too, showed that he is fully equal to anything that may be asked of him in an international match. He is still young to be a New Zealand representative, a clean player, if ever there was one, and is still a star in the line-out in which he took the ball more frequently than anyone else on the ground. (*New Zealand Times*, 8 September 1923)

The Last Word (With A Touch of Icterus)

The three newspapers devoted a good many more column inches to discussion and analysis of the match, but the most succinct, yet comprehensive, and to some extent differing, critique comes from the pen of 'Tackler' in NZ *Truth* of 8 September:

**'ASHES' REGAINED
NEW ZEALAND'S SWEEPING VICTORY
SUPERB FORWARD WORK
VISITORS' DISAPPOINTING DISPLAY**

The All Black team of 1922 was avenged at Christchurch on Saturday last, when New South Wales went down to the elect of New Zealand to the tune of 34 points to 6, and the 'Ashes' once again found a resting place in the Dominion. The weather was ideal and the playing surface at Lancaster Park was in first-rate order, there being only one or two patches where the grass had failed to stand up to a hard season's play. The game proved to be a most disappointing one, and with the exception of the opening stages of each spell, was a very one-sided affair, and well below the standard of international Rugby.

Again the balance of weight was in favour of New Zealand. The All Black pack averaged 13st 9lb per man, as against 12st 11lb of New South Wales. Then again reach was also to the advantage of the home side, Pringle's six feet four being of inestimable value in the lines-out. ['lines-out' – lovely word – there's proper grammar for you!]. Though mostly a forward game, it was not so much so as in the first test at Dunedin the previous week. In that match the black forwards were called on to do their own part and the backs' share as well. It was a different tale at Christchurch. The backs carried the confidence of their vanguard and never at any stage of the game was there the least suggestion that the confidence was not warranted.

Though not a brilliant set, the home rearguard was solid. The way the whole of them got down into the 'hard stuff' when it happened along was the bright feature of their play. The first spell gave nothing to indicate that there was to be a rout in the second half. At the interval there was only 13 points difference between the pair, three tries, all the result of loose forward rushes.

With the first ten minutes of the second spell left behind, the black forwards got into it in real earnest. They simply bashed their way through the blue team. There was no stopping them. They played like men possessed, and the up to then not too sure Cornstalk defence tottered and then crumbled. Of course the inevitable happened. There was try on try, some the result of magnificent play and some the outcome of the blacks getting away with infringements that the referee failed to detect. With monotonous persistency Sinclair hoisted the flag after each try, never mind what the angle be. At odd times Davis rallied his henchmen and, with Marrott, attempted to turn the offensive, but his efforts were always short-lived. There was too much individualism and not enough team-work.

With play at fever heat things became at times a little willing. In the tight a whole lot of actions not covered in the rules were noticed, and it was lucky for some of the offenders that their indiscretions failed to come under the eye of the referee.

From a spectator's point of view the game was a cruel one to watch. The average spectator wants to see the home team the victors, but he also wants to see the opposition put up some sort of fight. Contrary to the wishes of the crowd, Richardson must have told his men to get a move on and annihilate the Bosward charges. Be that as it may, there is not the least doubt that the blacks over-ran and overwhelmed the blues in the second spell, and at times it was pitiful to see half the NSW team strewn in the wake of the invading army of General Richardson. [Oh, to have been there, and not shed a tear!]

One was spellbound at the magnificent play of the black forwards. They could be likened to a battering ram opposed by a strawboard gate, such was the defence made to appear. In their mass formation the silver fern men never lost the ball. One man had it at his toe, and when he lost it there was always two, nay three, to carry on. Such tactics would test to the utmost the best set of defensive players in the world. Then, just to show they were not there for the benefit of their health, the backs would join in and harry the far from happy blues. They did not attempt to do anything spectacular, the good old chain pass being always to the fore, and so ground was made and most often a black player finished across the line.

The pace was tremendous – killing is the word. Only the fittest of fit could have stood up to it. The closing stages demonstrated which was the fitter of the two. And it was not New Zealand that stopped. In fact, they were going more strongly over the last bit than at any other stage of the game.

After the first test an improvement was looked for in the New Zealand team, but there was no reason to believe that the NSW backs would fail to put up a fight. For when one gets down to tin tacks, that is where the game was won and lost.

> Playing under the worst of disadvantages – lack of weight – the blue pack gave a great display under the circumstances. Their backs wanted the ball; the forwards saw to it that they got it far more often than the black half. On Dunedin form things should have been lively. They were. In fact the black backs had quite a lively time in getting in among the lob passes. Efforts that were born with the greatest of promise were short-lived and in most cases died horrible deaths.
>
> Practically the last thirty minutes of the first spell was made 'tight'. The black vanguard had the big stick there. The wearing down process was in operation. NZ was helped (not intentionally I hold) by the referee ordering scrums for a held ball. Energy, so precious to them, was expended by them as a result of this unfortunate mistake. Once the referee had to issue a general warning to the forwards. The hard stuff was then delivered in the tight.
>
> The end came at last. It was very thankful to all, players and spectators alike.

Speaking as a Kiwi, one finds it difficult to accept that any New Zealand spectator would be 'thankful' to see the end of a match in which Australia (or anyone else for that matter) was on the receiving end of such a hammering at the hands – and feet – of the All Blacks! 'Tackler' was evidently more critic than fan, although after the Wellington match his quite lyrical encomium hinted at the opposite being the case.

Back to 'Tackler':

> After the match Mr T.H. Bosward stated that he was disappointed in the result, but he admitted that on the day there was 'only one team in it'. Alf. Griffiths was the most pleased man in the world. Richardson, the winning skipper, was also highly delighted. Captain Sheehan said, 'Fair and squarely beaten by a better team.' He also had a word to say about [how] much 'yapping' [*Encore plus ça change*] there was, and as the match progressed the talking grew till at last the referee was compelled to speak to Sheehan about the way his team were using up good breath. [Well, there's Cornstalks for you ...]

New South Wales v. New Zealand – The Third Test: A Tactical Selection

Having seen the 'Ashes' regained, the selectors lost no time in carrying out their plans for the third test, with 1924 in mind. This from the *New Zealand Times* of 2 September 1923:

> **THE THIRD TEST**
> **NEW ZEALAND TEAM**
> **EXPLANATION BY MR S. DEAN**
>
> The twenty players from whom the New Zealand team for the third test match will be selected were announced last night by Mr S.S. Dean of the New Zealand Rugby Union. He explained that the selection of a new team was not due to dissatisfaction with the second test team, but to the selectors' desire to obtain the best team available in New Zealand for the English tour next year.

None of the 20 was among the 16 (including Brownlie) who played in the second test. The new loose forwards included Cupples and the 19-year-old Stewart, of whom more later.

The All Blacks completed a clean sweep by winning the third test at Wellington on 15 September 38-11.

Thus, at the conclusion of the 1923 international rugby season, Nugget had won an All Black cap, played an important part in a winning side, and fully justified his selection both as a team man and as a player. With a bit more luck, without a cauliflower ear and a tactical selection, he probably would have won one or two more caps. But his season was not over. A week later he was in action again for Wellington at home against Otago.

CHAPTER 7

Back to the Day Job

Wellington v. Otago, 8 September 1923, Athletic Park

Once again we are spoilt for choice, with five newspaper reports to hand. On this occasion we will permit ourselves to cherry-pick from four and conclude by quoting extracts from 'Tackler's typically pithy account. From the *New Zealand Sportsman* of 8 September: 'Ideal conditions prevailed … the visitors were reinforced by Stewart and Williams, and Wellington had their best team in the field' which was:[1]

---

1 The names in italics won All Black Jerseys – more than half the team.

WELLINGTON

Malcolm
Svenson, 'Doc' Nicholls, B. Gibson
F. Tilyard, M. Nicholls
H.E. Nicholls (captain)
Porter (wing)
C.B. Thomas, A. Thomas
Pringle, McCrae, *Moffitt*
Hepburn, Osborne

The *Evening Post* confirmed that after a long and strenuous tour Otago were minus seven players through injury and reinforced by the two All Blacks from Dunedin. They lined up as follows;

OTAGO

Scott
Webb, Stewart, Wise
Gilberd, McDougall
Glengarry
Knox, Owen, Dickson, Duncan, Williams, Campbell,
Coombs, Milne.

Back to the *Sportsman*: 'The visitors kicked off with the sun in their faces.' Nugget played a very active part in what proved to be a one-sided game. In the first half: at 7-0, 'the Wellington forwards forced play back, **Pringle** in particular playing a great game, and Otago's line was in danger'. And in the second half: 'On resuming, Otago attacked strongly, Gibson getting Wellington out of an awkward situation. Smart passing by the local backs brought play on to Otago's line, **Pringle** being nearly over.' At 18-6: 'The game was enlivened by some bright play by **Svenson** and **'Doc' Nicholls**, and an opening was made by **Porter**, who sent on to **Pringle**, to **Moffit**t, and big Jim pushed his way over the line.'

The *Times*, however, saw that one differently: '**M. Nicholls** … tried a pot, a beautiful effort, which dropped short. Stewart caught the ball, but dropped it and put in a speculator, which went into **Pringle**'s arms He gave **Porter** possession and the wing cut infield to pass to **Moffitt** who shot over by sheer weight.'

And the *Post* has it as '**Pringle** enabled **Porter** to pave the way', and the *Dominion* as '**Pringle** and **Porter** handing the ball to **Moffitt**' without other comment on the preceding play but concluded 'the burly veteran lock boggled his way through three or four tacklers to a try.' 'Boggled' – what a lovely word![2]

The *Times* of 10 September reported:

---

2 'To boggle' is not in the ODNZE, but is in the OED, where it is given a different meaning: 'to be frightened, to shy or start away, or to handle clumsily or bungle' – quite the opposite of the usage here.

> A crowd of between 8000 and 9000 witnessed the final interprovincial fixture to be played at home this season. The game was a poor one, marred by many mistakes, and the Otago men had bad luck at times. Wellington, with the advantage of the weather, led in the first spell by 10 points ... to 6. [What weather, one might ask, other than the sun?] As play commenced, Webb returned **H.E. Nicholls**'s kick and from a line-out the Wellington backs went into action. A sensational burst by the Wellington forwards carried on, but the **Thomas brothers** and **Pringle** overran the ball. ... **Gibson** and **Pringle** were prominent in an attack. [At 7-0:] Battles in the line-out saw **Pringle** come through, side-step [!] Wise, and send to **Osborne**, who was pulled over [i.e., tackled. For not wishing to tackle an on-rushing Nugget, Wise was particularly well-named.]

The *Evening Post* thought the same: '**Pringle** shone out in excellent light when he jumped for the ball, and securing it set off for the line. He side-stepped an opponent [accorded anonymity this time] and passed to **Osborne**, but further progress was stopped.'

The *Dominion*, which earlier had opined '[a]mong a good set of forwards, **Pringle** and **Porter** were always aggressive' went one better with '**Pringle**, who for the major part of the game was the most noticeable of the home forwards, executed a very clever move. Following his own kick and putting his own men on side, he secured the ball high in the air, shook off a tackler and passed to **Osborne**, who was grounded. It was a fine individual burst.'

Back to the *Times*:

> [Still at 7-0,] 'a penalty saved the Wellington line. Play went the other way at once, Gilberd finally lining just as **Pringle** dashed up. Line-out work saw **A. Thomas** and **Pringle** both fail to take the ball when a try seemed certain; but after a stoppage **H.E. Nicholls** secured from a scrum and sent out to his brother **Mark**, who crossed near the corner flag but could not convert'

In the second half at 13-6: '**Svenson** broke through in sensational fashion. He passed to **Pringle** [who thus must have kept pace with the All Black winger] who gave him back the ball, seemingly in a forward pass, and the wing-three-quarter ran over under the posts. **M. Nicholls** converted.' However, according to the *Evening Post* and the *Dominion*, it was **A. Thomas** who took and gave those passes (but the *Post* also thought the return pass forward) – and the *Sportsman* saw it as being **'Doc' Nicholls** – but not forward!

And the final score against a by now no doubt dispirited team: '**Gibson** handled in turn, **Porter** coming round to take the last-named's pass, and as he crossed the Otago men didn't bother to chase him, as he walked round between the posts' (*New Zealand Times*, 10 September 1923).

The *Dominion* focused first on 'Demonstration Against Rough Play':

> A demonstration was made by the crowd on the terraces at an incident that occurred in their proximity at the western end of the ground, in which a Wellington player appeared to strike at an opponent, with whom he was grappling on the ground. The Referee, Mr H. Leith, said subsequently that he had not had occasion to warn any player and that there was nothing untoward in the incident.

In the match report in the same journal more details were given: 'Just before … half-time … a Wellington player [another accorded anonymity!] was tackled by Webb on the western line, and from the grand-stand one hundred yards distant it appeared as if the Wellington man delivered a blow at his opponent. The crowd expressed their disapproval.' 'Tackler', writing in *NZ Truth*, saw it as **Gibson** v. Glengarry! And the *Evening Post* was content with 'a Wellington back showed his disapproval of a late tackle in a manner that did not please those who saw the incident'. Handbags, obviously.

The *Dominion* concluded with the following: 'Mr H. Leith was the referee. His interpretation on the off-side rule did not always meet with approval from the crowd, who expressed the view that Wellington were given the benefit of many doubts when a more exacting referee would have declared them off-side.' No other journal commented on the referee's performance.

And so to 'Tackler', this time wearing his critic's hat, in *NZ Truth* of 15 September 1923:

A POOR GAME
WELLINGTON WALLOP OTAGO

There have been a few uninteresting games on the Athletic Park this season, but last Saturday's game was easily the worst of the year. It was a terribly one-sided affair, with Wellington always having the whip hand. The teams were fairly evenly balanced in the matter of weight, the advantage, if any, being with the visitors. At half-time the score was 10 to 6 in Wellington's favour, but in the second half the home forwards went mad and simply swamped the opposition. At the call of time the Wellington score had advanced to 26 while Otago had failed to make any alteration to their total.

In the first half Wellington tried to make it a back game, but the rearguard failed to show that machine-like action so evident in the NSW fixture. It is just as well for Otago they did not, as, with any sort of combination at all, there would have been a cricket score. The defence offered to Wellington's attack was feeble in the extreme. Brainy play was not needed to score; clean handling would have done the trick. But pass after pass was dropped or mulled by Tilyard and 'Doc' Nicholls. [You can feel the man's frustration!]

In the second half spasm [now there's the word of a man in pain!] the Wellington captain changed his tactics and elected to make it a forward battle. It was a wise change. The home cavalry took charge and most of the half had matters all their own way.

> Generally a first rate pack, the Otago forwards were mere novices at the game as compared with their opponents. In every department were they outplayed, and especially was this so in line-out work. In this phase Pringle stood alone. [Tackler reckoned the lack of a 'decent kicker' cost Otago 'easily ten points'.]
>
> Both sets of backs when attempting a passing movement tore across field and thereby killed any chance the wingers ever had. Wellington were the main offenders in this respect and the sooner the inside men learn to run straight the better for our football. Nowadays the wing man is more an ornament than anything else when it comes to offensive play. Only two backs on the Otago side showed any inclination to give it a go. They were Wise and Stewart. As in attack there were only two who would get down – Wise [except when it came to Nugget!] and Glengarry. The remainder were satisfied to try and intercept or to go around the neck.
>
> The match was played in the best of spirit, there being only one regrettable incident, that when Gibson lost his 'nut' and punched Glengarry in the first spell. The bank saw the incident clearly and told the offender in unmistakeable terms what they thought about it.
>
> The Wellington scrum packed better than ever before this season and for once we did not see the hookers coming out through the roof of the scrum. Still, there could be a little more weight given in that back row.

In another column in the same issue, 'Tackler' wrote: 'Improving with every game is Pringle, the tall Wellington forward. He nearly reached the moon a couple of times on Saturday last when jumping in the line-out.'

Here Nugget's season came to an end. The Wellington team went on a northern tour, playing Auckland, Waikato, Wanganui and Manawatu, but he was not included in the squad. Presumably he was unavailable – possibly resting his ears! And his prospects for the 1924 tour? In an uncredited cutting, 'Old Blue' wrote an article entitled 'Our Rugby Laurels – Forward Tactics – And Other Factors':

> Undoubtedly New Zealand's victories over New South Wales were due to superior forward play, but it must be realised that their superiority in weight and physique gave them a natural advantage. … For a well-balanced scrum in our formation the two front-rankers must be of short stature and in consequence they are more often than otherwise much lighter than the other members of the scrum, and we lose a quota of weight on this account. Skill in line-out play is as essential almost as the scrum. … In my opinion one of the best in this department to-day is West of Taranaki. … Pringle and Cupples have the height necessary to make them especially useful, and it is absolutely essential that three or four forwards who stand inches higher than their mates be chosen for the overseas tour.

And this in the *New Zealand Sportsman* of 22 September:

> ### HOMEWARD BOUND!
>
>  A well-known football authority who saw nearly all the important matches in New Zealand this season contributes to this paper the following list of players as being worthy to represent New Zealand at Home [Note the capital H!] next year: – Forwards: Pringle (Wellington) [13 names in all, including wings, together with 14 backs].

Raising high hopes, indeed. Nugget has become a hot favourite for the tour.

The Waratah's Farewell

The New South Wales team's tour ended with a 14-6 defeat at the hands of Wairarapa-Bush in Masterton on 18 September. Of the ten matches played, they had won but two (against South Canterbury and Waikato) and lost ten. The management, unsurprisingly, was not entirely happy.

THE WING-FORWARD CONDEMNED BY MR T.H.R. BOSWARD
MASTERTON, 19 SEPTEMBER

[Mr Bosward,] speaking at the complimentary dinner tonight, expressed the hope that the New Zealand Rugby Union would abolish the wing forward. There was no doubt, said Mr Bosward, that men like Bellis, Porter and Donald were spoiling good football, and he felt sure that the wing forward would not be taken kindly to when the All Blacks visited England next year. He was not an asset to the game, but a spoiler of good football. It was far better to play without bordering on infringements all the time. [How many of today's loose forwards would agree with that one?!] New Zealand was standing behind New South Wales in no uncertain manner as far as Rugby was concerned [well – we know what he meant – at least we think we do!] and he expressed thanks for the wonderful treatment in New Zealand, and felt bound to admit that the unbounded hospitality of the New Zealand people had proved too much for the team, and in some cases contributed to their defeat. (*Evening Post*, 20 September 1923)

Well – perhaps that's the nub, because: In describing the tour as disastrous, Greg Growden (*Inside the Wallabies*, p. 21) wrote: 'One player was prompted to remark on return to Sydney, "we would enter each town with a raucous blare of trumpets and sneak out again in the dead of night". Perhaps pre-match hospitality contributed! In the longer term, Mr Bosward was to have his way. While All Black and Springbok forward power dominated for most of the rest of the decade, the wheel turned as it always does, and by the 1930s the running game was proving winning rugby, while the wing forward was banned in 1932.

Summer, 1923–24

Nugget's leisure activities in the 'off-season' were not limited to cricket. He found success in the athletics world also. 'Starter' in his 'Amateur Athletics column' in *NZ Truth* of 8 December 1923 wrote:

> 'Starter' has noticed Nugget Pringle, the well-known Rugby forward, at most of the athletic meetings this year. Many Rugby backs have taken up sprinting and are benefiting thereby, and this scribe suggests that many of our fine forwards of the Pringle type, would get valuable training and exercise by taking on the shot-putting, javelin and hammer throwing, etc. With the many splendid forwards we have in winter there is no reason why these summer events should be practically confined to policemen as at present.

And according to the *Evening Post* of 11 December 1923:

> **AMATEUR ATHLETICS**
> **A GOOD EVENING MEETING**
>
> New competitors were seen in the shot-putting event, the winner turning up in the Wellington and New Zealand representative footballer, A. Pringle. … Putting the Shot: – A. Pringle (7ft), 38ft 8in, 1; D.O. Brown (scr) 37ft 10in, 2 …

In the scrapbook is the Wellington Amateur Athletic Club Order Form for 'Engravable Goods to the Value 15/-' for first place in the shot putt at the Combined Clubs meeting at Athletic Park, dated 11 December 1923. We do not know whether the money was ever spent, but it appears unlikely, as the form, although stained and folded, remains intact, the tear-off section 'to be retained by the firm' still attached. Nugget kept up an interest in athletics throughout his active life, and in another cutting from the *Free Lance* in 1943, he is seen, smartly dressed, 'stooping as he helps with the measuring tape at a sports meeting'.

THE SECOND TEST, 1.9.23

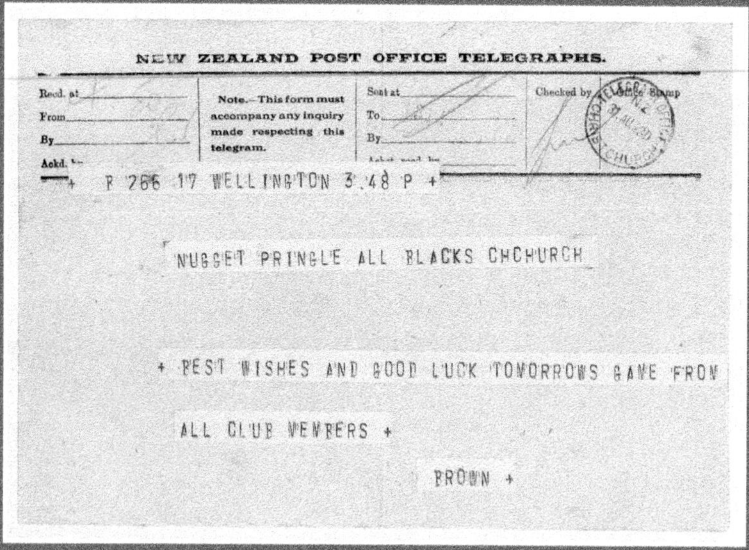

NEW ZEALAND POST OFFICE TELEGRAPHS.

R 266 17 WELLINGTON 3.48 P

NUGGET PRINGLE ALL BLACKS CHCHURCH

BEST WISHES AND GOOD LUCK TOMORROWS GAME FROM ALL CLUB MEMBERS

BROWN

Figs. 20 & 21. Good luck telegrams.

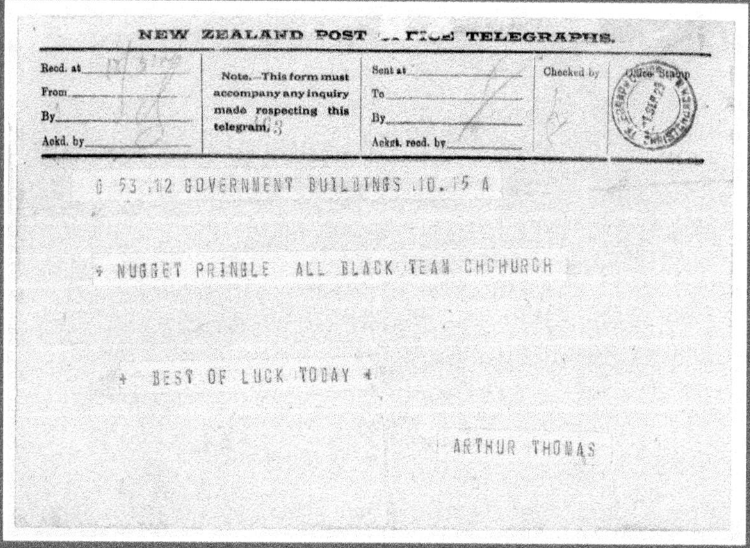

NEW ZEALAND POST OFFICE TELEGRAPHS.

G 53 12 GOVERNMENT BUILDINGS 10.15 A

NUGGET PRINGLE ALL BLACK TEAM CHCHURCH

BEST OF LUCK TODAY

ARTHUR THOMAS

Fig.22. Second test All Blacks. Note Nugget's headgear. "Back row – D.McMeeking, E.A.Belliss, L.McLean, A.West, J.Brownlee (sic), R.Sinclair, Q.Donald, W.Irvine. Middle row – W.Peina, R.J.Lucas, L.Peterson (sic), L.Williams, J.Richardson, A.Pringle, A.Griffiths (selector), M.Bell, W.Potaka. In front – W.A.Ford, M.Perry, P.J.McCarthy, H.E.Nicholls."

Fig.23. Second test Waratahs. "Back row – Mr T.H.Bosward (manager), W.J.Marrott, R.Elliott, E.J.Thorne, J.G.Blackwood, H.C.Taylor, R.Loudon, A.R.Erby, Mr T.Fletcher, (New Zealand representative). Front row – D.J.Erasmus, W.G.George, A.R.Armstrong, W.B.J.Sheehan (capt), T.S.R.Davis, R.G.Stanley, O.E.Nothling, N.Mingay."

Fig.24. Before the second test. "New South Wales gives three cheers for New Zealand."

Fig.25. Before the second test. "The New South Welshmen concluding their war-cry."

Fig.26. Action from the second test: "THIS IS NOT ANOTHER SALUTATION, BUT ERASMUS (NEW SOUTH WALES) ATTEMPTING TO BULLOCK HIS WAY PAST POTAKA (NEW ZEALAND). PRINGLE, PETERSON, AND BELL (NEW ZEALAND) ARE HANDY."

Fig.27. Action from the second test: "A PRECARIOUS POSITION: MINGAY (NEW SOUTH WALES) ATTEMPTS TO SNAP THE BALL AWAY FROM THE GIANT NEW ZEALAND FORWARD PRINGLE. BELLIS AND RICHARDSON ARE LOOKING FOR DEVELOPMENTS."

CHAPTER 8

1924 A Time of Trials

From the beginning of 1924 all rugby minds and eyes were focused on the forthcoming northern tour.

The 1924 All Blacks Tour

If you felt sorry for the 1923 Cornstalks with their stormy Tasman crossing and crowded month-long itinerary, think again. In this case 29 players and a manager were to embark on an odyssey many times as arduous. For starters, a party of 23 players were to set off across the Tasman on 27 June for a four-match series including three 'tests' against NSW, before returning to New Zealand in mid-July. There were then matches against Auckland and Manawatu-Horowhenua to be played on 23 and 26 July before the full party set sail for the United Kingdom.

The itinerary there consisted of 28 games including four tests commencing on 13 September against Devon at Devonport and culminating with the one against England on 3 January 1925. For afters, the team was off to France for two matches including one test in mid-January, and thence to Canada for two games in Vancouver and Vancouver Island in mid-February, before setting sail for home. This comes to a total of 38 games and at least six sea voyages – no mean undertaking.

When it came to selection, and with domestic competition not starting until the end of April, time was at a premium, resulting in a very congested programme of championship and trial fixtures. Nugget, typically, was not going to give less than 100% to either. He began in the autumn with the spring still in his step, in fine form and try-scoring mood, almost invariably being mentioned in despatches.

The annual report and balance sheet of the Oriental Rugby Football Club shows that the past year's activities have been attended with satisfactory results. ... Members have reason to be proud of our worthy club mate, A. Pringle, who, during a couple of years with the club, has risen from junior to the highest honour the country can offer any footballer, i.e., wearing an All Black jersey, and we hope that this year again will see 'Nugget' in the same position as that which he occupied last season. ... The club is in a sound position, there being a credit balance of £90 6s 6d. The club is now almost in a position to pay off at any time the £100 mortgage held on the gymnasium. (Annual Report, Oriental Rugby Football Club)

Oriental v. Petone, 5 April 1924: Won 16-9

As *NZ Truth* of 12 April reported: 'The football season was opened semi-officially in Wellington last weekend when five senior matches were played, the proceeds of the gates going to the gymnasium funds of the clubs. At Petone the local lads were downed by Oriental to the tune of 16 to 9, but the result was not a surprise to close followers.' And as the *Evening Post* (7 April) reported in more detail, 'the Petone backs [were] without the services of H. and M. Nicholls, who were playing in the cricket final'. Although they still had 'Doc'!

From an unsourced cutting we have a third match report on a

> very fast game which was played from start to finish.... The visitors were very slow to begin and for a time it looked as if the Petone supporters and punters would have an easy win, but they reckoned without the veteran skipper of the Orientals, Jim Moffitt, and when he gave his team a rally in the second spell, they rose to the occasion and scored their 16 points without turning a hair. ... Pringle was, as usual, in the foreground, and as well as being a scorer was a great

> asset in passing rushes. ... Jim Moffitt[1,2] would be a great loss to the team.

In a preview of the forthcoming club competition, *NZ Truth* of 3 May wrote: 'Nugget Pringle will, of course, be seen out once more, and as a prospective tourist great deeds may be expected of this rattling forward.'

---

1   *A word on Jim Moffitt*: James Edward 'Big Jim' Moffitt (All Black #222) was, like Nugget, an Oriental and Wellington stalwart for many years. There the physical similarities end. Born in Waikaia on 16 March 1887, Jim was 12 years older than Nugget, and at just under 6 feet tall and a full 15 stone, 5 inches shorter and a stone heavier. Nonetheless, the pair, working in tandem, ball in hand, at their feet, or bent on a tackle, must have presented a formidable prospect to the opposition. Jim first represented Wellington in 1910–12 and 1914–15 and helped lift the Ranfurly Shield in 1914. Rising to Second Lieutenant in the Auckland Infantry Regiment in WWI, he played for the New Zealand Division in the Somme Cup tournament in France in 1917, before helping New Zealand Services defeat 'the Mother Country' in the final of the King's Cup in 1919. With other members of the King's Cup team he toured South Africa with the Army side later that year. Back home, he toured Australia with the All Black side in 1920, and in 1921, now aged 34, locked the scrum in all three tests against the Springboks. He continued to play for Wellington until 1926, totting up 42 matches over 17 seasons. Moffitt served on the management committee of the Oriental Club in 1920–24 and 1938, was club captain 1932–36, and was made a life member in 1939. He died in Auckland on 16 March 1964. What a giant! One can only speculate on the rapport and camaraderie which must have existed between the two men, but what a vast amount of knowledge of the game must Nugget have acquired from Big Jim. (Bob Luxford, 'Player Profiles', New Zealand Rugby Museum)
2   A former gold-mining town in central Southland, Waikaia, apart from excellent fishing, boasts a museum and a house constructed of 20,000 wine bottles. With the population unchanged at 99 in both the 2006 and 2013 censuses, this works out at approximately 200 bottles for each man woman and child.

He did not have it all his own way, however.

Oriental v. Petone, 3 May 1924: Lost 3-13

This was 'Ories' first game of the season, after a bye the previous Saturday. Although it was lost, according to the *Evening Post* '[a] feature of the game was the good form shown by **Moffitt**, **Pringle** and **Brown** for Oriental, and Thomas and King for Petone'. However, *NZ Truth* saw it differently:

> Many that came to scoff remained to pay out when Oriental met Petone on the Athletic Park last Saturday. It was supposed by many that Oriental's pack, including Pringle and Moffitt, would suffice to turn the tide against the suburban backs, and there were other tales abroad to the effect that Oriental were, in fact, the dark horses this season. … Matt Love, the Petone lock … working like a Trojan … had it over Jim Moffitt. … 'Nugget' Pringle didn't show his best either. It was noticeable that Rice … the new man from Poverty Bay, made Pringle his especial mark. He sorted him out for his own, and in the line-out was always marking the long fellow. Rice is no midget himself, and a first-rate forward to boot, so that Pringle's lustre was dimmed accordingly.

From this point Nugget's season became very demanding, if not hectic, as he played club and trial games virtually alternately, two matches a week.

Oriental v. Old Boys, 10 May 1924: Won 18-0

> A more one-sided game ... could not have been witnessed anywhere last Saturday. ... Pringle, the big six-footer, although awkwardly built [interesting – the first we have heard of this. Awkward for his opponents, anyway!] was a whole heap of strength in the scrum. On two occasions he made good use of his height and fell over and scored six points for Ories. Many of the public have it that Pringle should be included in the 'All Black' team. (*New Zealand Sportsman*, 17 May 1924)

The *Evening Post* of 12 May gave his tries a bit more flavour: 'From another line-out later, Pringle secured and dashed across to score ... 3-0' at half-time, and 'immediately on resumption, Pringle got the ball, and an effort to prevent him going over the line for a try proved futile ... 6-0'. An unattributed cutting, clearly published on 15 May 1924, reads:

ABOUT PLAYERS

The two most outstanding players last Saturday were Moffitt and Pringle, in the Oriental pack. ... Pringle is simply a demon in the line outs. He gets the ball almost every time, and bullocks his way through the opposing pack. Both these players are big, and they take a deal of stopping when once they get away. When they are stopped they have the strength to raise the ball above their heads, and throw it out to the backs – just what a good forward should do. I see that both men are nominated to take a place in the game tomorrow at Wanganui. Pringle, in my opinion, is a certainty for the All Blacks. He scored two tries against Old Boys.

Nugget's First All Black Trial: Wanganui, 16 May 1924

The *Evening Post* of 12 May 1924 names the Wellington players (ten in all, including Nugget) 'nominated [by the Wellington Selectors] for places in the combined Wellington-Horowhenua-Wairarapa-Bush District team to meet Taranaki-Wanganui-King Country at Wanganui on Friday next', while that of 13 May confirms Nugget's selection for the starting XV. The following day the *Post* gave an account of the travel arrangements: 'The Wellington members of the team are to leave for Wanganui by the New Plymouth express tomorrow morning [and] are expected back in Wellington *in time to take part in the club matches on Saturday afternoon*' (i.e., the following day – emphasis added).

In the scrapbook is a telegram from Wellington, received in Wanganui on 16 May that reads as follows:

> A. Pringle
> Wellington Trial Football Team Wanganui
> Best of luck today
> Jack King

And on the same page an undated note:

> Best of luck 'Nugget'
> A. Corley

Prior to the match, the *New Zealand Times* carried a critique of the selection of the Wellington combined side:

> **WAS IT THE BEST**
>
> [N]o one more than the players themselves will be agreeably surprised if many of them are included in the redoubtable twenty-nine. To say the back-line is poor is to understate the case. … As to numbers, Wellington has no cause to complain. … Moffitt, the selectors seem determined to ignore. Pringle, of course, could not be ignored, and it may be anticipated confidently that he will be in the ultimate selection.

The teams were as follows:

WELLINGTON-HOROWHENUA -WAIRARAPA-BUSH

Full-back: **N. Walters**
Three-quarters: **R. Booth** (Wai.), **K. Svenson**, **H. Carson** (Wai.)
Five-eighths: **F. Booth** (Wai.), **M. Nicholls**
Half: **H.E. Nicholls**
Wing: **C. Porter**
Forwards: **J. Swain**, **Q. Donald** (Wai.), **A. Pringle**, **I. Harvey** (Wai.), **S. Willoughby** (Wai.) *Planned replacement by **A. Thomas** at half-time
R. McAnulty (Bush), **R. Moynihan** (Horo.)

TARANAKI-WANGANUI-KING COUNTRY-MANAWATU

Full-back: J. Sinclair
Three-quarters: J. Bailey, H. Brown, G. Hart
Five-eighths: P. Potaka, P. Byrne
Half: T. Baddeley
Wing: E. Belliss
Forwards: M. Symonds, H. Galpin, A. West, W. Ross, R. Pattersen, P. Carroll, W. Geange

We have long cuttings on the game from the *Dominion* and the *Times*, both dated 17 May 1924. Each carries an almost identical Press Association (PA) account of 16 May of the match itself, followed by a telegraphed report of the same date from their own 'Special' correspondent, commenting on the players. First, a summary of the PA report:

> **WELLINGTON WINS BY NARROW MARGIN**
> **SOME BRILLIANT FLASHES**
>
> "There was fine weather, and an attendance of about 6000. On a dry ground the game was much faster than the previous trial game in Auckland.[3] [...] Play was keen and hard, with a wealth of incident, although neither side showed much cohesiveness in attacking work. [...] The standard of individual play was good [...] The game was lively from the outset, with both teams endeavouring to get their backs going. *[With the half-time score standing at 7-3, (two goal kicks, including one drop-goal, to a try), several substitutions were made, but Nugget played the full game.]* The game became fast and spectacular on the resumption, each side attacking in turn [...] Both sides were making the game open, and the ball was thrown about in good style, but infringements constantly spoiled moves that promised well."

Thus it was a very open game throughout, and the narrative largely recounts back play, as in the second half the northern team scored a converted try to take the lead, to which Wellington

---

3 The first trial, involving players from the northern half of the island, including Hawkes Bay, had been played in Auckland 6 days earlier.

replied with two tries, one converted. It ends: 'Both teams showed signs of tiring in the concluding stages.' Not surprising, considering it was only the third or fourth game of the season!

"Dropkick" in the *Evening Post* of 17 May reported that in the second half, with the score 10-8, 'the lead was further increased per medium of a loose rush by the Wellington trio, **Porter**, **Pringle** and **Thomas**, the last named gathering up the ball and dashing over.'[4] Towards the end the northerners scored another converted try, following which '**Pringle** and **Harvey** set out after that for another score, but the opposition turned the attack' to leave the final score Wellington Combined 15, Wanganui Combined 13.

"Dropkick" concluded by saying 'When the bell signalled the end of the game the spectators crowded to congratulate the players on their splendid performance…For the racing enthusiasts in the town the game provided excellent sport for their off day.'

---

4   During the football season, from 1901 to 1938, "Dropkick" contributed regular discerning, enthusiastic and on occasion passionate Saturday columns on the game to the *Evening Post*. For many years, including Nugget's era, 'Dropkick' was Reg (Rex) Hornblow, Sports Editor in his day, and on the staff from 1910 until his death in 1947, apart from WW I service. The identity of the equally talented "Tackler", who wrote in similar fashion for *NZ Truth* in the 1920's, remains a mystery. (Ron Palenski, personal communication.)

How They Shaped: Comments on the Players

> The outstanding player ... was Porter. He played a splendid game, clean and hard, and quite over-shadowed his vis-à-vis Bellis. Bellis was inclined to rely too much on tactics which are not required of our representatives in England [Now, isn't that a delightful way of putting it?!]. In the forwards, Pringle, Swain and Harvey were the pick. All three played solidly and were going well right through a very tough game. ... The Wellington team return by the Main Trunk train in time for their club matches. Any further team should include ... Pringle [and ten other names]. (*Dominion*, 16 May 1924, by telegraph)

The *New Zealand Times* reporter opined:

> To begin with, there was no forward who stood out as West, of Taranaki, did. West is no infant to the game. ... He spent so great a percentage of the afternoon on the ball that he seemed to be the oval's appendage. ... Next to him among the men of the scrum came Pringle, of Wellington. In fact, he may have been the equal of West, so well did he play, but one cannot dispose of the stern fact that West is a man who has stood the test of time, whereas Pringle is yet proving his worth. Pringle's advantages are several. He has height, reach, weight and enterprise, and given the others, enterprise is the greatest of all.

Interestingly the *Dominion* made no mention of West, saying 'Paterson and Carroll were the pick of the north forwards, and Ross played a fair game', and not including West in its 'further team' selection. For what it is worth, the *Post* of 17 May agreed with the *Dominion*: 'Porter was the best forward on the ground. … Pringle was, on his game, easily among the best five forwards.' And *NZ Truth* (24 May 1924) concurred:

> Next to Porter, the most outstanding player on the field was Pringle [Note: not just forward, but player] the elongated Wellington forward. It took him a few minutes to get going, but once under way he played a magnificent game. Literally, as well as figuratively, he was head and shoulders above the rest of the forwards engaged. He tore into the game like a man possessed, and though naturally most of his work was seen in the open, he toiled every bit as hard in the tight.

Bully for Nugget, then, by general agreement – a first test passed with honours, one would have thought.

That same evening (i.e., 16 May), the selectors announced the Possibles and Probables teams for the next trial at Athletic Park the following Wednesday, 21 May, with Pringle named as a 'support' in the Possibles starting XV. West joined him as 'breakaway'. The teams were made up solely of players from the North Island, and this event was to be followed by the North-South game on 31 May. At that point the seven selectors would name 16 'certainties'. The other 13 places were to be contested by the remaining candidates in a second Possibles-Probables match on 3 June, only three days later. Meanwhile, there was more club football on the agenda.

Oriental v. Poneke, Saturday, 17 May 1924: Won 13-11

A great game it was, full of incidents and spectacular play, finishing with little difference between either team. King was a 'dark horse', coming to light by securing all of Oriental's aggregate through excellent kicking. [This with a strong wind blowing the length of the field.] Pringle, owing to the after-effects of his match at Wanganui, was not up to his usual form, being rather sluggish in his movements. [Hardly surprising.] Ories scored all their points in the first half with the wind at their backs, and won by four goal-kicks to three tries. [The irony was that King, Ories' captain, was] erstwhile one of the shining lights of the Poneke team. (*New Zealand Sportsman*, 24 May 1924)

Possibles v. Probables, 21 May 1924, Athletic Park

POSSIBLES (in black)

Full-back: **Walters**
Three-quarters: **Lucas, Svenson, Kirwan**
Five-eighths: **Cooke, Badeley**
Half: **Wright**
Wing: **Belliss**
Hookers: **Swain, Q. Donald**
Lock: **Harvey**
Supports: **Pringle, McLean**
Breakaways: **West, Moynihan**[5]

PROBABLES (in white)

Full-back: Nepia
Three-quarters: Grenside, Brown, Hart
Five-eighths: Johnston, Paewai
Half: Mill
Wing: J. Donald
Forwards: Irvine, Lomas, Righton, C. Brownlie, M. Brownlie, McNab, Knight

Again we have the benefit of two reports, one from the *Dominion* of 22 May, and the other unsourced but probably the *New Zealand Times*, also 22 May. The latter provides the more detailed account. From the *Dominion*:

---

5 Sinclair, Mark Nicholls, Porter and Cupples, were originally named in the starting XV, but withdrew; Sinclair at full-back having declared himself unable to make the tour and Porter through injury. More of Cupples anon.

> **POSSIBLES DEFEAT PROBABLES**
> **A HEAVY SCORING MATCH**
> **OPEN AND SPECTACULAR PLAY**
>
> The conditions were ideal … it was an Indian summer afternoon, … [with] scarcely a breath of wind [and] 9000 spectators. … So evenly were the teams matched that the result was in doubt right up until 'no-side' was sounded, and the swing of the pendulum in the closing stages had excitement and enthusiasm at fever heat. [Wow!]

In a nutshell, this was a match in which the lead changed hands five times, and each side scored four tries. A Probables potted goal by Nepia took the lead 21-20 late on, but the Possibles replied almost immediately with a McLean penalty from two yards inside half-way to win the match 23-21.

A few snapshots from the *Times*: Midway through the first half, with the Probables leading 8-6, the Possibles' tactics were changed. The inside backs,

> **Wright**, **Badeley** and **Cooke**, all fast and resourceful, kept the ball near the centre of the field, and when near the line exchanged passes with those of their forwards who were fast enough to be alongside them. **Swain**, **Q. Donald** and **Pringle** were easily the fastest. By these tactics two tries were scored before half-time,…

(making the score 12-8 to the Possibles).

> **THE SECOND SPELL**
> **PACE MAINTAINED**
>
> Those breathless movements in the first spell, in which back after back handled the ball at high speed were in the mind of the spectator as the teams filed onto the field after the spell. The pace of the play during the first half had often been terrific. Could they keep it up? They could and they did. The spell opened in electrical fashion…

As for Nugget, his 'mentions in despatches' related to taking part in 'determined' and 'slashing' forward rushes.

How the Players Shaped Up

The *Dominion* reported that: 'The honours of the day rested with Nepia.' Of the Probables forwards, 'M. Brownlee [sic] was one of the best forwards on the ground. … C. Brownlee and Lomas were the pick of the remainder.' For the Possibles: 'West, Pringle, Swain and Q. Donald were the pick of the vanguard, and all worked conscientiously throughout.' Are we damning with faint praise here? 'It was a tribute to the condition of the players that they lasted the great pace at which the game was played from start to finish.'

The *Times*, by way of contrast, felt:

> There was no better forward on the ground than Cyril Brownlie … there was little to choose among the others. … M. Brownlie was his brother over again, except that he was not as fast. … The Black forwards, as a whole, were inferior to the opposing pack. … **West**, **Q. Donald** and **Pringle** were slightly superior to their fellows, and of the three, **Donald** did the most work.

From the archives, 'Tackler', writing in *NZ Truth* of 24 May, reached similar conclusions in his article 'A Game to Remember', but had a little more to say. He also rated Nepia as the outstanding player and thought the Probables forwards superior. '**Pringle**, as ever, kept at it and was heading the rushes all day. … M. Brownlie was responsible for a marvellous game. … C. Brownlie was good, *but a forward who uses the questionable tactics this one does is better on the bank*' (emphasis added – remember the 1923 Ranfurly Shield game?). 'Tackler' concluded: 'The most bright incident, however, was the tackling. It was of the one and only get-down order and the Possibles' line, without exception, showed out.' A curious turn of phrase, but methinks we get the drift!

The *Evening Post* of 22 May noted that all but one of the players had appeared previously in the Auckland and Wanganui trials, the former having taken place on Saturday, 10 May, six days before Wanganui. 'Some of the players were handicapped by having played two games (including one trial) at the end of last week, and it was noticeable that those who were conspicuous in the game at Wanganui were outshone by others yesterday'. Nugget may well have been one of those. The Hawkes Bay contingent had played in Auckland.

In this context, 'Tackler's comments on the Auckland trial are both amusing, and, in the light of subsequent events, highly relevant. The match was played between Auckland Combined and Hawkes Bay Combined teams, and on heavy ground the Auckland backs gave the big but as yet unfit Hawkes Bay forwards the run-around, resulting in an 18-9 victory for Auckland. 'Tackler' wrote:

> [B]ig heavy men … like big horses … need a terrible lot of work before they can show their best form. M. Brownlie played a whale of a game. …He was fighting for his side, and, at the same time, fighting fatigue. It was a close go, and fatigue just won. C. Brownlie was a very tired man with the game two-thirds through, and he was loafing at the finish. Cupples wanted a chair early in the piece and he wandered around following the play with as much interest as a blind man at the pictures. He will have to get stuck right into training if he wants to go Home. McNab went longer than any of his team-mates. He was always with the ball.

NZ Truth of 24 May 1924 also carried the selection of the North Island team. In the starting XV, the Brownlies were the 'side supports', with Pringle in the back row alongside McNab. Three days later, and Nugget is back with the Ories.

Oriental v. Selwyn, Saturday, 24 May 1924: Won 12-3

An unsourced, undated cutting sets the scene: '[A] muddy playing area … and a very uninteresting game.' With his team 6-0 up, '[a] nice piece of dribbling by Pringle put Oriental in their opponents' territory, where, from the ruck Watts passed to Evans who was successful in scoring' making it 9-0 at half-time. 'When the combat re-started', the teams scored an unconverted try apiece to make it 12-3. 'Without anything of further interest the game finished with the scores unaltered.' Oh dear! Not a happy day at Wakefield Park unless you were an Ories supporter. Another unsourced cutting reports that Jim Moffitt was absent, and that 'Ted' King had an 'on' day with his kicking.

> The Oriental back combination ... was wonderful. The old axiom "unity is strength" may be applied to members of this Oriental fifteen, who work together like one big family of brothers. Poulter and Pringle were always conspicuous in the forwards, the last-mentioned being the one responsible for the score secured by Evans. ... For the major part of the first spell, Selwyn were without the services of a right wing three-quarter, but as this phase was nearing a close, Pegley came on and satisfactorily filled the gap.

Well, that must have helped a bit. However, 'Drop-kick' in the *Evening Post* of 31 May did have this to say:

> The tall, rangy 'Nugget' Pringle played a great game for his club against Selwyn on Saturday, and despite the slippery and uncertain nature of the turf, he was always on the ball and looking for work. On several occasions he secured possession of the leather and cantered down the field on his own, but many good chances were missed through lack of support.

Possibly relevant to the last was that Big Jim was out with an ankle injury. In the same article, published on the day of the inter-island match, but before the outcome was known: 'From a close observation of form in representative and other fixtures during the past few seasons … as well as giving weight to followers of the game [in various parts of the Dominion] … "Drop-kick" suggests the following as the best twenty-nine … who have appeared in the trials.' His 'sides and back row' were the Brownlies, Cupples, White, Richardson, Pringle, West and Belliss, and his locks Masters and Williams.

On the same day, 31 May, and under similar circumstances 'Tackler' undertook the same exercise in *NZ Truth*. He had seen 'all the trials to date'. His 'sides and back row' were again the Brownlies, Cupples, Richardson (Southland) and Pringle, together with, in his case, McNab and McLean (Auckland). Harvey and Williams were his choices as locks. Thus, with two trials still to play, Nugget was still a hot favourite for selection in the eyes of these pundits.

In the week following the Selwyn match, Nugget had no more rugby prior to the inter-island fixture. Instead, the chosen 44 were to assemble on Thursday, 29 May in a Wellington hotel, where they would undergo medical tests, and stay until the final trial on Tuesday, 3 June. The chosen lucky final 13 would be named that evening.

North Island v. South Island, Saturday, 31 May 1924, Athletic Park

The teams were as follows:

NORTH ISLAND

Full-back: **Nepia**
Three-quarters: **Lucas, Svenson, Hart**
Five-eighths: **Cooke, M. Nicholls**
Half: **Mill**
Front row: **Irvine, Q. Donald**
Lock: **Harvey**
Side supports: **M. Brownlie, C. Brownlie**
Back row: **Pringle, McNab**
Wing-forward: **Porter**
Emergencies:
Backs: **H.E. Nicholls, Paewai, Brown**. Forwards: **Lomax, Knight, West**

SOUTH ISLAND

Full-back: Fairbrother
Three-quarters: Steel, Robilliard, Gilmour
Five-eighths: McGregor, Perry
Half: St George
Hookers: McCready, Munro
Lock: Masters
Supports: R. Stewart, Richardson
Back row: White, Turpin
Wing-forward: Parker
Emergencies:
Backs: Dally, Elvey, Bell. Forwards: Williams, Tunnycliffe, O'Regan, Blick

A cutting from the *NZ Sportsman* of 31 May 1924 is the only one we have on this match, and, although it carries no match report, let us address it first, if only to listen to our correspondent's wonderfully exuberant language, as we quote him verbatim:

NOTES ON PLAYERS
HOW THE FORWARDS SHAPED

To individualise in an important game such as was witnessed this afternoon – the most important match incidentally for twenty years – is an exceptionally hard task for any man, be he selector, journalist, or the man on the bank. No matter what opinions are expressed there will be critics – more or less authoritative to dispute your dictum. That being so the following notes written from personal observation of the game this afternoon must not be taken as recording the pragmatical assertiveness of the writer – after all whose opinions may be apocryphal – but merely as the opinions of one who but expresses the views of many who will be chronicled as witnessing what will go down in history as an historical contest.

> It is the writer's intention to deal particularly with the forwards. ... M. Brownlie is a splendid specimen of the bustling forward type and gave an exceptionally good display this afternoon. With his brother – another outstanding figure – he may be already said to have the All Black label on his back. McNab proved himself to be one of the finest forwards the team possesses. He is a good solid lusty player. Pringle showed himself to be a good solid hard worker and he was always on hand and in the thick of it. He reminds one of Alf. West and his lineout work. Can be put down as a passenger for the trip home. Incidentally he is in the pink of condition if his play this afternoon is any criterion.
>
> As regards the South Island pack ... Richardson was undoubtedly the hero of the South Island side and on today's play must be a moral for the final thirty. He put in some great lineout work and lived up to his reputation as being one of the greatest New Zealand forwards playing in the Dominion today. Richardson has only to consult Cooks for any further particulars! Stewart, although only a very young player, displayed most uncommon promise this afternoon. He used his head and will be a valuable acquisition to the final thirty when the names are announced. As regards White: this player is not as young as he used to be, but nevertheless he toiled consistently hard this afternoon. A solid man.

Which, of the loose forwards, leaves only poor Turpin deemed unworthy of mention. Stewart, incidentally, was but 20 years of age, and curiously, was also born in Waikaia – Jim Moffit's hometown.

Turning to the archives, the *Evening Post* of 2 June, two days after the game, carried a match report, from which we gather the following. The game was watched by a record crowd – over 18,000 people – 'tier upon tier on the western bank'. The conditions were good, with rays of sunshine,

> until clouds gradually banked up from the south [and] in the closing stages of the game ... a heavy rain shower, with hail, was experienced, but that was not the only disappointing feature of the day. Contrary to expectations the game was such a one-sided affair that it tended to dampen the crowd's enthusiasm, though a plentiful supply of incidents, mainly from one side, kept the onlookers well interested and entertained. ... On each side, South and North, there were great forwards, well worthy of international status, and there were also backs who promise to be worthy successors to those who made New Zealand famous on the Rugby field. ...
>
> Shortly after the appointed time the teams marched on to the field in single file, and their appearance was the signal for an enthusiastic demonstration [they then] paraded in front of the official stand and gave three cheers for the Prime Minister (the Right Hon. W.F. Massey). The members of the Boy Scout Delegation to the British Empire Exhibition, who were guests of the New Zealand Rugby Union, followed with a haka. Attention was then directed to the field of play.

> Luck ... went against the Southerners, who lost the toss, and had to face a northerly wind in the first spell and a southerly on changing ends. ... [I]t soon became apparent that the sides were unevenly matched. ... [T]he northern backs gave a splendid display, working so well together and showing such cleverness that they completely outclassed the opposition. The battle between the two packs was more even, and while a certain amount of brilliancy was shown in the loose, the scrummaging left much to be desired.

The half-time score was 25-0, and the final score 39-8.

Given such a one-sided encounter, a more detailed account of the run of play would get us no further. Suffice it to say that Nugget did not get a mention, that M. Brownlie 'played an exceptionally fine game', while the 'South backs were failing badly, both in attack and defence, but the forwards played up gamely, and Richardson, White, Parker and Stewart did their best to retrieve the waning fortunes of their side'. The *Post*'s 'Notes' had this to say (with knowledge of the chosen 16, one must add):

> One of the best features of the game was the high standard of play shown by the forwards in the loose. Richardson and White stood out as top-notchers. ... Although on a badly-beaten side, they were the two best forwards on the ground, and were justly entitled to the honour bestowed upon them by the selectors. Once again the two Brownlies were very much in the picture. M. Brownlie appeared to better advantage than his brother. ... The two locks, Harvey and Masters, were below par in their particular work in the scrums, but otherwise they played well, putting in a lot of useful work, as also did Pringle and Turpin [ah – a mention for Turpin at last]. Pringle, with C. Brownlie, made good use of height in the line-out. McNab toiled away consistently. Last but not least of the forwards is Stewart. His form was splendid, and he has earned his place in the New Zealand team.

As a weekly journal, published on Saturdays, *NZ Truth* in its 7 June 1924 edition carries in separate columns accounts of each of the final trials, and on the final selection. As far as the inter-island match went, 'Tackler's views on the forwards differed from that of the *Post*, and then some!

The most one-sided inter-island match ever played. In the annals of the game never has such a crushing defeat been inflicted. After [the 1921 Springbok tour] the North Island started to experiment with a new type of player – the big man. He has taken a few years to perfect but on Saturday last we saw the finished article. And what a splendid type of manhood he is! He is nearly [sic] six feet high, can gallop like a back, has the weight, and what is most important, the brains. He has every right to be known as a super man. He is the equal of any forward this country has ever turned out. In the South things have not taken this somersault. … One man – Richardson – set them the example, but his type was never copied. … Last Saturday the North forward in the tight was the equal of his Southern opponent; in the loose he was infinitely superior; and in brainy work he was head and shoulders above the southern man. … Irresistible is the word that describes the play of the Black jersey [i.e., North Island] men. …

In a loose scrum how many times did a North forward obtain the ball and pass back to his rearguard as compared with the South? About ten to one. In a line-out who tipped the ball back to his half the more oftener [sic] – North or South? North by a large majority. Another piece of play the North forwards came at on several occasions was the short pass. When the forwards come at a short passing stunt they start a movement that is one of the hardest in the world to stop. Only at hooking did the South pack shine. The South front row pair hooked like clockwork and if any of the team helped to keep the score down it was Munro and McCleary. Had the North received their fair share of the ball from the scrums the score would have been in the region of sixty.

As for individual players, 'Tackler' had this to say:

> Grand is the word that describes M. Brownlie ... as fast as a deer. ... Let him produce this form at Home and the critics will go into raptures over him. C. Brownlie is not in the same class as his brother, but [he] was a good second to Maurice on Saturday. ... *Cyril has one bad habit and he will have to drop it pronto. He is inclined to go for a man when he has got rid of the ball. This can easily be mistaken for dirty play and at Home he will find himself in hot water if he should come at it. Drop it once and for all is the author's advice.* [emphasis added]
>
> In such company as he was surrounded Pringle did not get a chance to shine, but he was there boots and all. In the line-out one did get a glimpse of him. Pringle is far yet from a polished player, but with the right handling he would be as fine a forward as Wellington has turned out for some time.
>
> McNab is honest and does not look for medals. If there were medals for toiling McNab would be up on the platform the day they were being presented. ...
>
> Even with the crook ankle that went on him in the second spell, Richardson was the best forward on the ground. ...
>
> Stewart was always in the picture till his ankle went and he is certainly going to be one of the forwards who will most benefit by the tour. ...

> After the Invercargill trial the writer thought that White was going down hill, but after his last Saturday's display I take it back. He is still a fine forward and one of the very few ... who knows anything about dribbling. ... Another thing – nobody would ever dream of saying that White is not honest.
>
> Turpin is not a New Zealand forward ... on Saturday ... he was outclassed.

After the match the selectors announced the names of their chosen 16 certainties. The Brownlies, Richardson, White and Stewart were in. Nugget still had more to prove. The *Post*'s 2 June issue also carried the teams selected for the final trial the following day (Tuesday). Pringle and Cupples were the Possibles sides, with Turpin and O'Regan at the back, their Probables opposites being Knight and West, and McNab and Snow, respectively. Of those, only Pringle, Turpin and McNab had played on the Saturday, O'Regan, Knight and West being on the bench and not called upon. West had missed the first Possibles-Probables game also, as, although named in the original selection, he was, in the event, replaced by Moynihan in the starting line-up. The *Post* added: 'The All Black certainties and possible and probable players will be the guests of the Wellington Rowing Club at the latter's birthday ball tomorrow night. The final selection of the All Black team will be announced during the evening.'

Possibles v. Probables – The Final Trial, Tuesday, 3 June 1924: A Damp and Muddy Squib

There being no cuttings relating to this event in the scrapbook, we must turn to the archives, both for a match report and for comments on the players. The teams were:

 **POSSIBLES (in black)**

Full-back: **Harris**
Three-quarters: **Elvey, Bell, Robilliard**
Five-eighths: **C. Badeley, Perry**
Half: **Dalley**
Wing: **Parker**
Forwards: **O'Regan, Turpin, Cupples, Williams, Pringle, Lomas, Q. Donald**

PROBABLES (in white)

Full-back: Nepia
Three-quarters: Bailey, Brown, Hart (replacing Svenson)
Five-eighths: McGregor, Paewai
Half: H.E. Nicholls
Wing: Jacob
Forwards: McNab, Snow, Knight, Masters, West, Tunnicliffe, Munro

The *Post* published first on 4 June:

[T]he holiday yesterday treated the All Black candidates and a much-interested public very poorly. The weather had been on its worst behaviour since [the previous Saturday. Because of the churned-up ground the curtain-raiser was called off, and the day was] wet and cold, with a very keen southerly bringing up rain squalls at intervals.

For the record, the Probables (in white) won 16-8, while the few accounts of forward play in the *Post*'s account include:

> Nepia's stout defence saved his side in the face of several dangerous attacks with the Black forwards dribbling well together. ... The Black forwards, particularly Cupples, were great in the loose. ... [From a line-out close to the line,] Turpin seized and fell over. [The score was 10-8 at half-time.] ... The weather changed for the worse ... for the second spell. ... [T]he game developed, accordingly, mainly among the forwards. Here Cupples was specially prominent among the Blacks in his excellent work in the loose. Time and time again, he was to be seen leading a forward rush, ball at toe.[6]

As for individuals:

> Of the other [i.e., other than locks and hookers] forwards it can only be said that several were on a par, with Cupples showing up as an excellent controller of the leather in loose rushes. West, Turpin and Knight were always conspicuous, and McNab and Pringle toiled away conscientiously, with a strong hand in line-out work. Pringle has had a hard row to hoe in the trials, and his performance from the time he started off with a fine display at Wanganui has been very creditable. O'Regan and Snow were useful assistants.

---

6   This the same Cupples who, less than four weeks ago, was so unfit he wandered around the field like a blind man at the pictures!

'Tackler' on 7 June wrote in NZ Truth of 'A MUD SCRAMBLE … heart-breaking to the men engaged in a desperately fought affair. … Briefly, it was a case of luck. … And, believe me, a player needed all the luck going to keep his feet after the first quarter of the game. … The Probables won [because of] the defence of their backs and the clean work of Nepia at fullback.' Of the players he thought: 'There were two outstanding forwards – Cupples and Knight.' No other loose forward earnt special mention. 'The remainder of the pack was always a very even affair. The lot were always going, and that says a lot. It was not a day to judge play, especially back play.'

The Lucky 13

That evening the Selectors announced the names of the 13 players who were to complete the touring party. West was to head North, and Cupples also had played himself in. Nugget's name was omitted. He was played out, in more ways than one. Again we must turn to the archives. Not surprisingly there was criticism of some of the selectors' choices, but on the whole general agreement that they had had a very difficult task, and taken overall, it was a pretty good team. This from 'Drop-kick', in the *Evening Post* of 4 June 1924:

> **SOME SURPRISES**
> **SELECTION CRITICISED**
>
> The New Zealand selectors … have done their work, and the result … will be received with mixed feelings. One thing is for certain, in choosing the final thirteen players they have not given the general satisfaction that was apparent after the announcement of their first coice [sic] of sixteen players. The team, as finally chosen, presents one very marked weakness. … The weakness referred to is in the full-back position. … Nepia has shown his versatility by doing the work of a full-back competently, but he has never yet been really hard-pressed in all the matches he has played, and his methods yesterday were, to say the least of it, perilous and more characteristic of his original role as a five-eighth.

In 'Drop-kick's opinion, a 'substitute full-back' should have been picked as back-up. 'What is to happen if Nepia is incapacitated?', he asked. His fears were unfounded. George Nepia, still only 19 years of age, played at full-back in all 30 matches of the European tour, and became both a legend and 'the face of the tour'. 'Drop-kick' continues:

> No great exception can be taken to the choice of forwards, though 'Drop-kick' holds the opinion that by his performances Knight (Auckland) undoubtedly played himself into the team. With so many forwards about the same merit, a little more consideration might have been given to youth. To the abundance of good forwards Pringle and others, with their careers all in front of them, must attribute their ill-luck in missing the trip. Harvey [a lock] is among the fortunate. Pringle is not.

The *NZ Truth* of 14 June expressed the view that 'the big majority admit that the selectors made a very good job of their assignment. ... In all they witnessed nine games and saw in action over one hundred and fifty players.' However, it took a different view of Nepia, who in the Auckland trial had played at five-eighths and 'was not worth notice, but on the Monday, as full-back, his display was the only feature of an otherwise drab affair'.

As an aside, the writer here is referring to the Te Mori Rose Bowl North-South Maori match, played on the Monday two days after the Auckland trial. It is amusing to note *NZ Truth*'s terse comments on 17 May after that game: 'A SHOCKING EXHIBITION ... one of the most drab games ... if any of the players engaged expect to get into the All Blacks they have more nerve than Ned Kelly. There was only a handful of people present, and those who stayed at home knew more than a thing or two.' Some words to be eaten there! Now, a month later, and by way of contrast, it went on to say that Nepia 'went one better' and 'played brilliantly' in the first Possibles-Probables match, was 'the central figure' of the North-South game, and 'in the last trial he also played magnificently. Nepia is a full-back who will electrify the bankers[7] at home.' Also, here's a nice one: 'Paewai must have come to Wellington in a coach drawn by a regiment of black cats, for he had more luck than a Chinaman to get in.'!

> To try and find fault with the Brownlie brothers, Richardson and Cupples would be a waste of time. They are men who will set the British Rugby world on fire. The country has never turned out such fine specimens of manhood, and no praise is too high for them. ... White is perhaps the most honest forward playing in New Zealand today. He covered himself with glory at Wellington in the North-South game. As an exponent of dribbling he has not a superior in New Zealand, and the funny thing about his work in this direction is that in most of his essays he comes through the pack with the ball at toe. No waiting in the loose for him. ... Last year Stewart was a fine forward, but he lacked the necessary weight. He has built up this season. He is a boy that the tour will improve one hundred per cent. ... And then we arrive at West. How does the old song run? Oh, Lucky Jim. It should read in this case lucky Alf, for if ever a man was lucky West was. A few years back West was perhaps the best line-out forward this country has produced, but his days are over. In 1920 he was the best man on the

---

7   'Banker' is, in this context, not a fat cat in the City of London, but a humble spectator. According to the ODNZE, 'the bank' is 'an earth embankment ... used as a grandstand in many New Zealand sports (especially rugby union) fields, and often associated with the rowdier spectators; by metonymy the "regulars" of the bank as a group. Hence 'banker', formerly, a spectator on the bank of a rugby union field.' Hence also 'to send (one) to the bank, to give an order for the bank, to send (a rugby player) off the field of play as a penalty'.

> Sydney tour. ... But this is 1924 and West is starting to slip. He is still a good man, but not a match for several who were missed by the selectors. ... There are several unlucky individuals kicking about the country at the present time. The place that went to West should have been allotted to Pringle, McNab or Knight. The last-named had a darned sight more right to it than West.

Why Did Nugget Miss Out?

There were those who were outraged by his omission, including 'Katipo'[8] (unsourced cutting) who wrote:

> The All Black tests provided a lot of material to 'chew the rag' about, especially as to the selectors' lack of vision in not choosing our Mr Pringle as being worthy of wearing an All Black jersey. In our humble judgement they have made a grievous mistake, which may well mean that they will go through without a single victory. We sincerely hope not, for that would be a dire calamity. Our condolences to 'Nugget'.

The bottom line, though, was that the selectors were spoilt for choice when it came to big fast forwards. However, there were other reasons why, in the space of a week, Nugget went from being hot favourite – indeed, a certainty in the eyes of some – to also-ran.

---

8   The Katipo spider is the only poisonous non-human creature in New Zealand, although its bite is rarely lethal. It is evident here, however, that, in human form, when aroused, it can be extremely venomous.

1. Inexperience

In marked contrast to 'Katipo', another writer, in an unsourced cutting but possibly the *New Zealand Sportsman* of 26 July 1924, saw things differently:

> Pringle just missed All Black honours. What was the reason? Where is the deficiency? Few forwards in Wellington or in New Zealand can equal him in his usefulness in the lines-out. But his defect is that, although at other times he battles hard, much of his energy is lost. This is particularly noticeable in tight work. He does not seem to appreciate where he can be most useful. The thick of the fight is not for him. In the loose, heading the rush, or stemming a rush, he does valiant service. He tackles well and hard (not rough) and takes the ball cleanly and with a minimum of mistakes. He is a valuable asset to the Oriental team ... in tight work.

Written two months after the team was selected, it may have been a time when Nugget was a little jaded, even disheartened, and lacking in enthusiasm. His reported performances in domestic games in June and July 1924 do indicate some 'loss of form' (see below). This does not seem like the Nugget we know, however, and if true, the defect may well have been due to inexperience. At the time, although 24 years old, he had been playing rugby for only two years and still had a lot to learn. By way of contrast, the 20-year-old Stewart had played three years of First XV schoolboy rugby before selection for South Canterbury, including against the Springboks aged 17 in 1921.

He also played in the third test in 1923. The other six chosen were vastly more experienced, ranging in age from 25 to 31, three of them WWI veterans.

2. Ill-fortune

He certainly had a 'rough row to hoe' in the trials. In addition to playing in all four in the space of 18 days, he faced foul conditions in the final match, while the walk-over in the North-South game cannot have helped his cause. Playing out of position as he was, it would have been difficult to stand out among the Brownlies and co. in such a picnic, while his loose forward rivals in the South team would have had more opportunities to shine when displaying 'stout defence' – as they did.

3. Injury

Part of the family legend has it that Nugget missed out because he was carrying an injury in the final trial. The *NZ Truth* of 14 June 1924, reporting on those who missed out, provides contemporary confirmation; 'Lock Williams was another stiff. He played with a crook leg (as did Pringle).' 'Racket' ('Rapid Rise in Rugby', 1939) gives this account:

>  [H]is omission caused a lot of surprise at the time. ... His was another case of the folly of a player taking part in a trial when a slight injury prevented him from reproducing the form of which he was really capable. So many players, however, go on to the field in a trial regardless of whether they may be in top gear, and at such times the selectors would be better advised to warn a man against playing. Pringle suffered a bruised thigh muscle and played in the final trial against medical advice. He had been showing form right through, but had a lapse in this game, and with it went his prospects of All Black selection.

4. Indiscretion

Did playing in the final trial with an injured leg against medical advice cost Nugget his place? Did the selectors know and take it into account? Or was he damned if he played and damned if he didn't (in which case he would have had no chance to prove his worth)? Given the conditions, and the displays of Cupples and Knight in the mud, that seems to be the likely truth of the matter. And one final thought – to what extent might the club games he played in that period (including that against Poneke the day after the Wanganui game) have fatigued rather than strengthened his already over-worked constitution. There is even mention in a later report that he suffered an injury in that first trial, which may have contributed to his poor game against Poneke, but which, given his later performances, does not seem to have been of lasting consequence. If true, however, it underlines still further Nugget's valorous determination to play on when discretion might have been the better course.

All one can say by way of conclusion is that Nugget missed selection for the Invincibles by a whisker, and that he was very unlucky to have done so.

Postscript: How Fared the Magnificent Seven?

According to the player profiles in the Rugby Museum:

Twenty-year old Ron Stewart, who went off with an ankle injury in the inter-island match and did not join in the Australian leg of the tour, continued to be troubled by injuries. He played in only ten matches at the start of the tour, and missed most of the second half, playing one game in Canada on the way home. However, he went on to an illustrious career as a player until 1930, and a selector until 1950. (Bob Luxford, NZRM)

Alf West proved the critics right. At 31 he was not in the league of the Brownlies, Cupples and Richardson, playing only ten games in Europe, two in Canada, and no internationals. (Lindsay Knight, NZRM)

Andrew 'Son' White, while only a year younger, became one of the most valued players on the tour. He was a regular for first team selection, playing in 28 games including three of the four internationals. He also found a role as a goal-kicker, scoring five tries and kicking nine conversions. (Knight, NZRM)

Johnstone 'Jock' Richardson took over the captaincy from Cliff Porter, who was injured early in the tour. He played in 28 matches, including all the tests, and was captain in 14. (Knight, NZRM)

Leslie Cupples MM,[9] a Tokaanu farmer, even 'though his selection was not universally popular, had a successful tour, playing in 18 of 32 matches', including two tests. Despite his giving the appearance of 'a blind man at the pictures' in the first trial, he was 'remembered by players of his day as a dedicated footballer who did his training before breakfast'. (Luxford, NZRM)

Cyril Brownlie played 20 games from Australia to Canada, including three tests, and won 'an unenviable reputation in rugby history [when] in the international at Twickenham, after an early skirmish, Brownlie became the first man to be sent off in a test when he was banished by Welsh referee, Arthur Freethy', leaving the team with 14 men. 'It appears that … though not entirely blameless, [he] may have been unlucky. The first offender seems to have been one of the England forwards, Edwards' (Knight, NZRM). Nonetheless, 'Tackler's forebodings came to fruition. The lad had form.

For the legendary Maurice Brownlie, 'the 1924 tour was a triumph'. He played in 30 matches including all four tests. His personal highlight came after his brother's dismissal. 'So furious was Maurice at the injustice he believed his brother had suffered he later picked up the ball and with an incredible display of power and determination carried several defenders over for what was a crucial try in the All Blacks' 17-11 win.' (Knight, NZRM)

Left Behind: The Rest of the 1924 Domestic Season

Seeking vengeance on Fate's fickle footballing fingers, Nugget was back on the park four days after the final trial – this time at the Basin Reserve.

---

9   Military Medal.

Oriental v. Athletic, 7 June 1924: Won 16-15

Let us begin with the *Evening Post* of 9 June, which, in a full account, had this to say:

> Athletic [even without their All Blacks] had a team reckoned strong enough to beat the 'Ories'. Let it be whispered that the same 'Ories' were very keen to beat Athletic, as the reply generous to the failure of the selectors to include in the All Black team one of the most popular Oriental forwards. ... The way they worked up and won by one point provided one of the thrills of the season.

In a later issue (14 June) and of the same game 'Dropkick' wrote: 'Pringle is taking out his disappointment at unjustifiable non-inclusion in the All Black tourists in the proper way by redoubled efforts to give his club another leg up.'

An unsourced cutting in the scrapbook gives a full account of what must have been an exciting game with a remarkable turn-round, played before a big crowd. The Ories are at times given the nickname 'the Magpies', and also called 'the whites'. The team sheet shows Big Jim locking with Nugget on the side:

ORIENTAL

King
H. Smith, Juno, Hume
Wilkins, Park
Chambers
Barr, Simmons, D. Smith, Pringle, Moffitt, Watts,
Hepburn, Brown

ATHLETIC

Brook
Sawtell, Cookson, B. Gibson
Carey, G. Gibson
Warwick
Smith, Swain, Osborne, Parks, Webb, Spencer, Adam,
McKernan

Ories kicked off and at once attacked, but the Athletic forwards sent play down-field. **King**, the Magpies' fullback, effected a good save and Brook also stemmed a sharp Oriental onslaught. A free kick to the blues saw play in Ories' 25 but the white forwards changed the venue and were dangerous until smartly stopped by Warwick, but a miss-pass gave Cookson and B. Gibson an opportunity which **King** just checked in time. Athletics [sic] continued attacking but a free kick gave the Magpies relief. A hard kick by an Orie forward saw the ball in Brook's hand and emulating Nepia he potted a goal from a good distance.

Athletic ... 4
Oriental ... 0

A free kick resulted in **King** finding the corner flag and Ories just missed a score. A force resulted and Athletics charged down the field. From several forwards the ball travelled to B. Gibson, to Cookson, to Sawtell who raced over. No goal.

> Athletic ... 7
> Oriental ... 0

Five minutes later from a pass by Warwick, B. Gibson ran through and scored. Cookson landed a fine goal.

> Athletic ... 12
> Oriental ... 0

A good run and kick by **H. Smith** put Oriental in an attacking position. A free kick by **King** was fruitless and a scrum ensued on Athletics line. Off-side play gave the blues relief; but the whites pressed the attack, the ball passed through all the backs, but a knock-on spoilt a good chance to score and Athletics were finally forced. Play hovered in Athletics '25 for some time, **Moffitt**, **Pringle** and **Simmons** being prominent. The Oriental backs again got going and **Chambers** by a dodgy [nice word that – nothing underhand of course!] run missed a score by inches. [What would they write these days – by centimetres? Ugh!] After play in midfield, Athletics again attacked hard and Sawtell, knocking on, missed a certain try. Then a series of passing rushes by the Orientals followed. **Chambers** was conspicuous in every instance and his smartness was finally rewarded by **Hume** touching down after a great run. **King** failed with the kick.

Athletic ... 12
Oriental ... 3

Two minutes after resumption, **King** had a shot at goal from half-way, the ball going just outside the post. Then he essayed a pot which fell short and **Simmons** had a shot from a mark which also missed. From these onslaughts, Athletics forwards carried the ball up-field and the backs taking a hand saw Gibson rush across. The attempt failed.

Athletic ... 15
Oriental ... 3

This set Ories attacking and from a determined forward attack **Brown** touched down and **King** goaled.

Athletics ... 15
Oriental ... 8

The whites again became aggressive and a kick up field brought them to the blues line where B. Gibson was temporarily knocked out. **Hume** raced round and a fine kick sent the ball out at the corner where Athletics gained respite with a free kick. Warwick earned applause for a clever bit of play which transferred operations to the whites' '25. The little half again got away with a dodgy [anything you can do] run and was within an ace of scoring. The blue backs again charged but **Pringle** got the ball at his toes and brought play to half-way. Good play by the Orie backs was followed by their forwards who had Brook guessing and in a twinkling **Watts** snapped up and dashed over. No goal.

> Athletics ... 15
> Oriental ... 11
>
> A great run by **Hume** was stopped by Brook and play went to the '25 line where **King** missed an easy penalty kick. Again **Chambers** got his backs away, and **Cookson** transferred to **Hume** who scored a brilliant try, which **King** capped by a beautiful goal.
>
> Athletic ... 15
> Oriental ... 16
>
> Orientals played safely and kept the blues in their own territory. A free kick saw **King**'s shot, from a difficult angle, hit the posts. Then followed a fruitless attempt from a mark and the blues transferred play to the other end, but their stay in the white's territory was short-lived. A mark by **Chambers** frustrated an Athletic charge and the game ended with play in midfield, Orientals being victorious by 16 to 15.
> Mr T.A. Fletcher controlled the game efficiently.

The *NZ Truth* of 14 June contains another full and similar account, but with a few noteworthy extras:

Ories played against the wind in the first half. ... Fat Porter and Svenson – 1924 tourists to Blighty – did not enter the playing arena, much to the relief of the Magpies, this being the very stimulus the doctor ordered. ... Ted King undoubtedly won the game by kicking a spanking goal. ... Strange it is but true, oh King! that Ted of Ories missed two very easy kicks and excelled in the devilish hard ones. ... Warwick behind the Blue scrum was as elusive as a Scotsman's saxpence [sic]. ... [And finally,] Pringle was not so conspicuous as is his wont, an injury affecting him. He should have been resting.

Which says it all.

The remainder of the domestic games of the 1924 season were less exciting and less successful overall for Oriental. The reports serve mainly to indicate Nugget's fluctuating form and fortunes during that time, before embarking on the representative season proper.

 **Oriental v. Wellington, 14 June 1924, Won 19-12: Another Win from Behind**

The *Evening Post*'s report on the same day says of the match: 'Oriental played a good game, and thoroughly deserved their win, although for a long time in the second half Wellington defended stoutly and kept a lead. Once they got the lead, however, Oriental piled up the points and won quite easily. ... Outstanding players were Pringle, Chambers and K. Smith for Oriental.'

Oriental v. Varsity, 21 June 1924, Lost 3-6: A Close Encounter of the Best Kind

The *New Zealand Sportsman* of June 21 contained a long report of another match at the Basin Reserve that 'drew a fair crowd of spectators to witness the game'. Nugget featured prominently:

> Hume got in a timely kick, and Pringle, following up, got within a few feet of the Greens' line … Pringle got away again, but Blathwayt stopped an ugly rush. … Then the Oriental forwards broke away and were frustrated in time by another game movement by Blathwayt. [What a nuisance that man is!] … Towards the end of the spell Pringle led another Oriental charge, but a threatened score was frustrated by Walpole. [And Blathwayt wasn't the only one!] … Moffit and Pringle were associated in some heavy forward work. Porter, a junior, made a great run, and was pushed out at the corner. … [With the score at 3-3,] Blathwayt earned applause for a brilliant save in his own 25. [Again! And so it remained until] the prettiest passing rush of the day. The ball was snatched by Hart, who sent to Walpole, to Britland, to McKay, to Riggs, who was held up on the line. Then Britland obtained possession and scored a well-deserved try. O'Regan's kick from a difficult angle fell short. Varsity 6, Oriental 3.
>
> The whistle sounded a minute after. Mr Kitto was the referee.

From the archives of the *Evening Post* (23 June 1924): 'Taking the game as a whole, a draw would have been a fair result. ... Juno, Chambers and Pringle were prominent throughout the game.' But *NZ Truth* of 28 June saw fit to add: 'Pringle and Watts were the hardest working forwards for Oriental. The former is a great asset in the line-outs, [What has become of lines-out? Sad] but is inclined to hang onto the ball over long when tackled.' The correspondent, who from the following could only have been 'Tackler', also wrote: 'The game was clean, and referee Kitto had it well in hand throughout. Once only was a fist seen to burst through the top of a scrum and land anything but caressingly on a receptive nose, but there was no means of knowing who the offender was. However, in these days of stirring football such are but the amenities of the fray.' Amenities? Aren't they defined as something intended to make life more pleasant or comfortable for people? And a final word from a *New Zealand Sportsman* cutting dated 28 June 1924: 'Pringle was again the life of the Orie forwards. Moffitt's accident [an ankle injury] in the second half toned him down a lot, but the other forwards never relaxed their strength or slackened their efforts – all of which shows that the Varsity forwards are a fine stamp too.'

 **Oriental v. Berhampore, 28 June 1924, Won 14-7: A Meat Pie for Nugget!**

An unsourced cutting dated 28 June 1924 carries an account of a relatively straightforward victory for Ories, whose pack 'was much heavier' than the other, and who led throughout. The scoring was opened when 'from a scramble on the line Pringle scored'. Later we read: 'Pringle's long reach in the lineout was of great assistance to his side' and that Big Jim was replaced when 'his ankle failed to stand the strain'. Furthermore, 'Mr

A.H. Leith gave every satisfaction with the whistle.' A nice compliment.

From the archives the *Post* gives Nugget's try a bit more colour: 'The driving power of the Oriental forwards was too solid on one occasion, and Pringle obtained a try when several opponents failed to hold him up.' While *NZ Truth* of 5 July took a somewhat jaundiced view: 'Better games have been played on the waving tussocks of Woop Woop's paddocks' and 'Nugget Pringle worked industriously throughout, without brilliance. *Nugget has lost his flair this winter*' (emphasis added).

 **Wellington v. Taranaki, 2 July 1924, Lost 14-9: A Mid-Week Trip Up-Country**

On Tuesday, 1 July, Nugget, with the rest of the Wellington side, took a break from the club championship and a train to Hawera for, on the following day, the first leg of the annual derby against Taranaki – a match which appears to have slipped under the scrapbook's radar other than for the announcement of the team selection. From the archives, *NZ Truth* (12 July 1924) informs us curtly that: 'At Hawera, on Wednesday, Taranaki defeated Wellington by 14 points to 9. The winners held the upper hand practically all the way.' Also from the Archives, the *Evening Post* (3 July 1924), tells us that the game 'was played … in fine weather, and on a good ground. There were about 5000 spectators. Taranaki proved a much superior team on the day's play, but the game was hardly up to representative standard. … The sets of forwards were evenly matched, but the Taranaki backs, having more opportunities, though not making the most of them, did sufficiently well to establish their superiority.' No individual forward was deemed worthy of special mention.

Three days later Nugget was back in action.

**Oriental v. Hutt, 5 July 1924,
Won 16-9: The Interceptor of Many ...**

The only cutting relating to this game is unsourced and dated 12 July 1924; it is the essence of brevity: 'Pringle was well marked on the field and was the tallest player. He was the interceptor of many a line-out throw owing to his height.' The archived *Evening Post* of 7 July carries a full report. 'A fairly interesting game ... hard and fast, but not of a spectacular nature. ... Mason and Moffitt did not turn out for Oriental, which team deserved its win on the day's play.' Nugget saved his best for last: 'Following another free-kick to Oriental, Christie and P. Sullivan made a good attempt to score, but Pringle cleared, the final whistle then sounding.'

**Oriental v. Marist, 12 July 1924,
Lost 3-5: A Conversion the Difference**

An unsourced cutting tells us: 'The absence of some of their best players – notably Moffitt and Hume – from the Oriental ranks last Saturday was the prime cause of their defeat. ... The forwards keenly contested the ball, the pick being Hopkins, McRae, Bowman and Griffin (Marist) and Pringle, Simmons, Watts and Hepburn (Oriental).' Which doesn't leave many! *NZ Truth* of 19 July confirmed that Brown also was absent and 'Oriental fielded a light pack ... Simmonds, who locked the scrum, is the only burly pack man, and his girth is of little use to the side in close work, and a positive handicap in the loose. ... Pringle played his usual solid game ... ably assisted by Poulter.'

In the *Evening Post* on 19 July, 'Drop-kick' told of a 'high wind sweeping across the ground … from corner to corner.' Oriental played against it in the first spell and 'their defence was sound' but their 'dash in the second spell seemed to have evaporated as a result of their hard work against the wind in the first spell. … Marist … were always dangerous … while each of their forwards was a "live wire", especially in the loose play, where they ran all over the Oriental pack.' The same journal had reported on 14 July that 'on one occasion Oriental had bad luck, a kick at goal crossing the bar high up being blown back by the wind and Sidel marked.' Another breezy day in Wellington. Each side scored a try in the second half, Marist's being converted by Murphy 'into the teeth of the gale'.

Wellington v. Wairarapa, 16 July 1924, Carterton, Lost 18-9: Up-Country Again – And a Meat Pie for the Reps!

This match also slipped under the scrapbook's radar, and again we turn to the archives. The *Evening Post* of 17 July 1924, under the headline 'Nineteen Attempts and No Goals' reported that it was 'fine weather, but the ground was somewhat holding. There was no wind, no sun, and no advantage in winning the toss.' Despite all this, Malcolm, the Wellington full-back, contrived to miss 19 goal kicks! In the play, Wairarapa were soon up 13-0 with three tries. 'The Wellington forwards began to show superiority in tactics in the line-out, and time and again set their backs in motion. … Pringle, McRae, Sullivan and company were identified in a dribbling rush' but all to no avail, and the half ended at that score. 'Penalties were given against Wairarapa repeatedly. Practically every scrum meant a free kick to Wellington, and mostly in good kicking positions', but all were missed. Late on, '[f]rom a line-out, Wogan scored [sic – secured?] and after a spectacular run, passed to Pringle, who scored. Gibson took the kick and failed. Time sounded with the score Wairarapa 18, Wellington 9.'

NZ Truth, under the headline 'Wairarapa Whack Wellington', reported on 19 July: 'There was only one team in it. ... It was thought by many that the Wellington team was a second-rate one. ... The forwards played as well as could be expected, but the Wairarapa van had it on them most of the game.' This suggests a much more one-sided game than the *Post* witnessed, while of Malcolm, *NZ Truth* thought: 'Malcolm, taking him all round, played a creditable game, but at times failed to do what was asked of him.' Such as kick goals, one might ask, though there is no mention of his failings in this respect. Rather: 'He was certainly up against it, as the Wairarapa forwards harassed the Wellington team considerably.'

Both these correspondents, I assure you, dear reader, were reporting the same game. However, it may be relevant, that 'Tackler' for *NZ Truth*, if it was indeed he, was taking an increasingly jaundiced view of the Wellington representatives' campaign as the season progressed. More of this anon.

 **Oriental v. Berhampore, 19 July 1924, Lost 14-20: Missing Personnel**

This was Nugget's seventh match in three weeks. Sadly, we now have reached the end of match reports in the scrapbook, with the exception of two later representative fixtures. The information we can draw from the archives concerning this and subsequent championship games is limited. The *Evening Post* of 21 July felt that: 'The Oriental team ... has suffered such losses in personnel that its future in the remaining games seems rather uncertain. Such forwards as Moffitt and Brown and backs like Chambers and Juno are out of it, for the time being at least.' Thus Berhampore were expected to win, and 'deserved to win by many more points'. Despite this, the half-time score was eight apiece, and Ories went on to lead 14-11 at one point, before succumbing to three late tries. In the *Post*'s 26 July issue, on the same game, it was reported that: 'The Orie forwards missed Brown and Moffitt badly, but held their end up very well. Pringle was conspicuous with some good work on [sic] the line-out and clever dribbling in the second spell which almost gave him a try', while *NZ Truth* of 26 July thought 'Pringle and Watts were easily Oriental's outstanding forwards'. Prior to this game, at the end of the first round, Oriental had finished second in the championship table, five points behind Petone. After this result Ories were overtaken by Berhampore and Poneke.

 Oriental v. Poneke, 26 July 1924, Lost 8-19:
Under Starter's Orders for a Nose Job

Jim Moffitt was back, but there was only sad news of Nugget in the *NZ Truth* report of 2 August:

 Nugget Pringle, Wellington's popular elevated forward, has received doctor's orders to have an injury to his nose attended to, and will very shortly go under an operation to have the defect remedied. This will mean that Nugget will be missing from Oriental's ranks for a period, but it is to be hoped that his recovery will be speedy enough to make his absence from football as short as possible.

The *Post* on 25 July did not list Nugget in the team for the following day, and on the Monday wrote: 'The Oriental team struck one as being lighter than usual, certainly in the forwards. ... Jim Moffitt stood out as the biggest man in the team.'

 **Oriental v. Marist, 2 August 1924, Won 6-3**

The *Post*, of 2 August, confirms that Nugget did not play in this match – indeed both teams started with 13 men, 'the vacancies being later filled by juniors'! Whether he had undergone surgery we know not, but, if so, his convalescence was brief, as he was back on the field the following week, after three weeks away, missing only two games. There is evidence presented later that he had his nose surgery the following year.

 **Oriental v. Wellington, 9 August 1924, Lost 5-10**

'Drop-kick' in the *Evening Post* of 16 August reported: 'The Wellington forwards were somewhat better suited to the heavy ground at Newtown than were Oriental, and clear evidence of this was furnished towards the end of the game, when Oriental were tiring fast. Pringle turned out for his club once again, and played a good game, though his height, on this occasion, proved more of a handicap than an advantage.' Curious!

**Oriental v. Petone,
16 August 1924, Lost 6-9**

'Drop-kick' again, in the *Evening Post* of 23 August:

> Oriental did very well to run Petone so closely. ... The town team hardly knew at the start whether they would be able to field a full fifteen. ... Jim Moffitt came out in a new role as wing forward, but did not make a sensational success of it. Moffitt is a born lock, probably the best in New Zealand. ... On the Oriental side Pringle had one of his best games, while the rest of the Oriental forwards made up a pack that quite held its own against Petone's.

Thus the club championship season came to an end, with Petone as champions, although the following Saturday they were beaten by Berhampore, the runners-up, in the play-off for the National Mutual Life Challenge Cup. For Oriental, a season which had promised much, saw them finish in fifth place. Now it was time for the representative season proper, commencing in Wellington, with the return match against Taranaki on 30 August. Nugget had been included in the 31 players called up by the selectors for training for the representative team, published in the *Evening Post* on 13 August, to start with a 'gymnasium practice'.

'Tackler's Lamentations 1 and 2, 30 August 1924

Lamentation 1

Here 'Tackler' bemoaned the current state of the game in New Zealand, which had been weakened, of course, by the absence of the 29 tourists.

> **IN TOWN AND COUNTRY**
>
> The 1924 season is rapidly dying and the big majority of enthusiasts will be very pleased when the final bell is sounded. There is no denying that the season has been a highly disappointing one. Only on rare occasions have we seen football that one could go into ecstasies of delight over. The play has been of a very poor standard generally speaking. ... The All Black trials took all the glamour out of club play, but ... should not be held ... responsible for the all-round deterioration that became pronounced once the All Blacks were selected. ... Public enthusiasm was at fever-heat till the All Blacks were selected, but with the twenty-nine men sorted out, the flame went out. Attendances fell off ... poor crowds ... teams drifted into a go-as-you-please style. Play lacked the vim and snap so necessary. ... Combination and science were forgotten and a mediocre style crept in. ... Certainly a small percentage of players lost heart when they found they had missed the bus for the tour, but that cannot be the reason.

'Tackler' had suggested that a second All Black team should tour New Zealand after the trials, but the 'suggestion was not acted upon (not that I expected it to be).' Rather, '[t]hat honour of late has been accorded to the Maoris, who only as recently as last year made a tour of both islands. Why the Maoris should be sorted out for this special privilege I do not know, but the fact remains that if the Natives are a good enough attraction for a Dominion tour the All Blacks would be doubly so.' He went on to say that with few 'star games' the West Coast of the South Island saw strong opposition from League and that in 'certain towns' generally 'there is a drift to League'. He had written a fortnight previously of several prominent players who 'were talking of going over', and was in 'no doubt' that League was 'making headway in New Zealand. ... That there is life in the League camp can readily be seen from the work its henchmen are carrying out.... No, League is not a spook. It is a fair dinkum live body living on the same oxygen as the Rugby counsellors.'

Lamentation 2

'Tackler's dim view of the 'Rugby counsellors' saw further expression in his second lamentation in the same issue: his preview of the Wellington-Taranaki match which was to be played that day.

> **PICKING 'EM**
> **SELECTORS' SHODDY SELECTION**
> **MISFITS, HAS-BEENS AND VAMPERS[10]**
>
> The Wellington team to play Taranaki at Athletic Park today was announced last Wednesday, and it caused a lot of gasping. When men of the wisdom of Messrs. Wallace, Buck and Wilson put their heads together one expects to see something decent as the outcome, but if the team to play today is the best possible the three wise birds can get – well, local football is at a lower ebb than I thought. The fifteen men to play, and the six emergencies, are a most variegated lot. There is a fair sprinkling of good men but the mis-fit, has-been, and vamper is also in evidence. How the selectors have managed to imagine some of those selected are worthy of rep. honours, they (the selectors) alone know. The Man in the stand and on the bank doesn't.

'Tackler' went through the team one by one, rejecting six, together with all the reserves! Among his comments are: On the unselected Hall: 'Hall was dumped for not attending a practice when not in a condition to do so.' On the selected Swain: '[Swain] is the champion vamper of New Zealand.' And

---

10 'Vamper' is not found in the ODNZE, nor is 'Vamp'. In the OED a vamper may be a stocking, someone who patches, or one who improvises on a musical instrument – none of which seem applicable in this context. In Partridge's *Dictionary of Slang and Unconventional English*, a 'vamper' may be one who picks fights in public houses in order that his mates may steal watches, purses and the like. Possible. However, 'vamp', noun and verb, is also defined as 'tramp or trudge', and although 'vamper' is not given this definition, it may be what Tackler had in mind.

on the Orie boys: 'Jim Moffitt is a light of other days. He can still lock a scrum, but that ends his usefulness. ... The two men on the sides pass muster, but Pringle has not played up to form for some time.' He ended the column with his own selection, which did not include Big Jim or Nugget, not even on the bench. Well, we shall see ...

**Wellington v. Taranaki, 30 August 1924,
Athletic Park: A Close-Run Thing**

Unsourced, that day, from the scrapbook, is the following.

WELLINGTON

Malcolm
Wogan, Mackay, Bedell
Johnston, Corner
Warwick
Fitzgerald
Thomas, Preston, Brown, Moffitt, Pringle, Shearer,
Swain

TARANAKI

Priar
Loveridge, Ennis, Ross
Johnston, Oliver
Jeffries
Fryday
Hunt, Robertson, Patterson, Baldwin, Kivell, Walters,
O'Rourke

[A]bout 4500 watched the game. ... The ground was on the soft side after recent rains, but the rain which had been threatening to come down had held off when the teams took the field. ... Wellington kicked off into a slight breeze and were soon on attack. ... A free kick sent play back ... **Malcolm** stopping a fierce onslaught. ... A passing bout between Johnston, Ennis and Ross saw the last-named make a great run down the line, but he was thrown out near the corner flag. The Wellington forwards forced play back and **Pringle** got possession and sent on to **Johnston**, who got over but was penalised for being off-side when he took the pass. **Wogan** was injured and left the field, **Lang** replacing. Taranaki had hard luck ... but were rewarded shortly after from a nice piece of back play, Ennis scoring a fine try. The kick did not increase the score. [An interesting way of putting it!]

Taranaki ... 3
Wellington ... 0

The next move was a fine run by **Lang,** who beat all the opposition, but the full-back, his pass in-field went a-begging. However, he was rewarded a little later by making an opening for **Mackay** to score. **Malcolm**'s kick hit the upright and fell on the wrong side. [Perhaps a slightly better way of putting it.]

Taranaki ... 3
Wellington ... 3

Taranaki set to with a will. ... **Mackay** attempted to clear with a kick but it fell right into Loveridge's hands who raced over. Ennis failed to convert.

Taranaki ... 6
Wellington ... 3

The local forwards headed by **Pringle** and **Shearer** were battling hard. ... [**Malcolm** just missed with] a great kick from just inside half-way. ... **Warwick** sent the ball out to **Johnston** to **Mackay** to **Lang,** who was crowded out on the line. [Play swung back and forth, the visitors giving] 'a bright exhibition of back play ... Ennis's centring kick being charged down by **Warwick** ... **Moffitt** broke through with the ball at his toe and Priar went down on it just in time. He was penalised for playing the ball on the ground and **Malcolm**'s kick at goal fell just under the bar. [The score at half-time:]

Taranaki ... 6
Wellington ... 3

[In the second half,] play went up and down at a fast pace and **Malcolm** badly mulled the ball, leaving Walters, one of the visitors' hefty forwards, to score a well-earned try. Ennis goaled.

Taranaki ... 11
Wellington ... 3

The reverse stirred the home team up and the best bit of passing of the day saw **Lang** score after the ball had been handled by **Warwick, Johnston, Corner** and **Mackay**. **Malcolm**'s kick went wide.

>Taranaki ... 11
>Wellington ... 6

The home team were throwing the ball about freely, **Mackay** spoiling several promising movements. **Corner**, with a great corkscrew run electrified the opposition and scored a pretty try. **Lang** failed with the kick.

>Taranaki ... 11
>Wellington ... 9

Another try looked certain from a run by **Lang**, who was playing the best game on the field. He knocked on, however, and Taranaki supporters breathed freely. ... **Malcolm** attempted a pot, but it was a poor effort and Ennis snapped up and closely supported by Kivell and Ross traversed the whole length of the field with short passes between them. Kivell got over the line, but the referee ruled he was off-side and a fine effort ended in nought. Wellington were straining every nerve. ... Priar ... was saving time and again. Taranaki were determined. ... A passing bout between the home backs saw **Lang** going strong for a try, a magnificent tackle by Priar getting him in the nick of time. ... Taranaki were penalised ... in a handy position, but **Malcolm** could not goal. After some tight play on Taranaki's line, **Pringle** emerged with the ball and sent on to **Mackay** to **Bedell** who scored the winning try, which **Shearer** [a hooker – Buggins' turn?!] could not convert.

> Wellington ... 12
> Taranaki ... 11

Time sounded shortly after with Wellington attacking. Mr A.C Kitto was the referee.

NOTES AND COMMENTS

Swain and Pringle were the pick of the home pack. Their following up proved them two players worthy of inclusion in any representative team.

'Drop-kick', from the *Evening Post* archives, wrote on 6 September:

> [I]t is now felt that local senior football is not as black as it has been painted. Wellington can produce the goods all right. ... A week or two prior to the match ... the selectors made a choice of players to go into training. Whether the choice was right is open to question, but the idea was right, and there can be no doubt that the good showing by Wellington last Saturday was due in no small way to the coaching and training which has been carried out in the gymnasium and on the field ... the form, of course could have been much better, but that which was shown furnished the selectors with a good reply to those who had criticised them harshly. [Like 'Tackler', 'Drop-kick' had been critical of the selectors' choice of players.] ... The teams were evenly matched. ... It was a good game. Taranaki fielded a very good team. ... Coming to Wellington's display, it may be said that it was very satisfactory. ... The Wellington pack played hard and well, doing their best work in the second spell, when Pringle was an outstanding figure. Moffitt and Preston were others who caught the eye ... but all went well.

And as for 'Tackler's lament, he wrote on 6 September of an 'exciting game. The visitors had a great forward pack ... but their backs were hardly up to the standard.' However, he was still not a happy man: 'Wellington's rear-guard was most disappointing, and five out of six of their passing movements ended on the line. Their forwards can also be improved. ... There are some who dodge the heavy stuff.' And of those he would have dropped, he wrote, without a word of contrition: 'Pringle was undoubtedly Wellington's best forward, and his line-out work was a feature of the game. The veteran, Moffitt, was full of dash, and at one stage of the game gave a neat exhibition of swerving, side-stepping and dummying as it should be done.'

Next on the block was Auckland, a match of which 'Drop-kick' wrote after the Taranaki game: 'A similar performance against Auckland to-day should be good enough to meet success.' And we shall see about that, too.

Wellington v. Auckland, 6 September 1924, Athletic Park

Another unsourced cutting dated 6 September 1924 carries the match report, and further evidence of a loss of public interest in the Game of Rugby.

> The weather and ground for this game were all that could be desired, but the attendance of 18,000 or 20,000 that in former times used to roll up for this match was not in evidence today and a modest 9,000 watched the proceedings. His Excellency the Governor General and party were present. Many of the Auckland players whose names are familiar to the rugby fans in big football were missing from the Auckland side today, nevertheless they fielded a fairly strong side. The teams were as follows:

AUCKLAND

Goodacre
Tonkin, Ifwerson, Kirwan
Maxwell, Foster
McManus
Anderson, McCullough, Palmer, McLean, Keene,
Webber, Keary, Batty

WELLINGTON

Walters
Lang, Mackay, Bedell
Johnston, Corner
Warwick
Fitzgerald, Haddock, Brown, Pringle, Preston,
Moffitt, S. Shearer, Swain

Auckland kicked off against a slight breeze and proceedings had not been in operation for many minutes before Webber was injured and was replaced by Knight. [Wellington, then Auckland, attacked, before] another casualty befell Auckland [and Maxwell was replaced by Loft. Auckland scored first, an unconverted try, following which play swung back and forth until] **Warwick** and **Bedell** put in a nice bit of play and long **Pringle** got the ball with his great reach and sent it out but the pass was forward and a try was missed. Wellington were rewarded shortly after as **Lang** landed a beautiful goal from a free kick.

Wellington ... 3
Auckland ... 3

The home team now warmed up and made things merry for a while. **Corner** sent out a long pass and **Johnston, Mackay** and **Lang** got going but Tonkin intercepted and showing a fine burst of speed looked to have a try in his keeping until he was overhauled by **Pringle**. [Not bad going, Nugget, to track and bring down a winger from behind!] Wellington were penalised, however, and Ifwerson made no mistake.

Wellington ... 3
Auckland ... 6

Half-time sounded with Auckland attacking hotly. ... [In the second half, Wellington started with a] fine movement by their backs [but **Lang** was] pushed into touch near the corner flag. ... A fine forward dribble by **S. Shearer**, **Fitzgerald** and **Pringle** took play onto Auckland's line, but the defence and tackling of the visitors left little to be desired. ... Some tight play took place on Wellington's line, but the forwards worked like Trojans particularly **Pringle** and **Shearer** and they saved their line from being crossed. ... The Auckland forwards were proving too heavy for the local pack and were getting the ball out of the scrums most times. ... A fast follow-up by the local team saw **Mackay** and **Lang** after a try, an Auckland player appeared to force down, but **Lang** picked up and was awarded a try [which he converted].

>Wellington ... 8
>Auckland ... 6

Excitement now ran high as Auckland strove hard to get the mastery. ... A free-kick to Auckland saw Ifwerson land a magnificent goal from just ten yards inside the half-way line and right out near the touch-line. It was one of the best kicks seen on the park for some time.

>Wellington ... 8
>Auckland ... 9

> The visitors were now having all the best of the play. ... Goodacre narrowly missed a pot. Time sounded shortly after with Auckland attacking. Mr Bradley held the whistle. The best team won on the day's play and Wellington were lucky to get out of it with only 1 point the difference.

So once again the blinds were down in Wellington. What did 'Drop-kick' and 'Tackler' make of it all?

> Wellington's performance was disappointing. ... It seemed to the writer that Auckland set out to beat the Wellington forwards, and early in the game they were given cause to believe that their idea was a good one. ... The Auckland backs [made] use of attacking kicks to support the forwards. These kicks usually differed from those made by the local backs in that they were executed in such a way as to be of advantage. ... 'This is the best forward team that Auckland has put in the field this season,' remarked a keen Auckland follower before the match. 'They are all workers; there are no vampers.'[11] ... Pringle was the best of the Wellington forwards, and Moffitt at times caught the eye as principal in starting off an advance. ('Drop-kick', 13 September 1924)

---

11 First 'Tackler', now 'Drop-kick'. It would seem 'vamper' was common parlance for a drone or slacker . See Note 10, p.185.

From *NZ Truth* (presumably 'Tackler') on 13 September came a diatribe with the headlines 'Wellington Well Whacked' and 'Though It Was Only A Point Victory': 'The old adage "Nothing Succeeds Like Success" cannot by any stretch of the imagination be fastened on to the shoulders of selectors of the Wellington reps. The only phrase the writer can see fit to pin on them is "Give Them Enough Rope", etc.' He went on to note that in 1924 Wellington had won only two games – one against weak opposition, namely Bush, and the other by one point, while in 1923 there were six lost, three won, and one drawn. 'The average citizen is only allowed to hold his job down while he can show results, but in the Rugby Union a man holds down his position by making as big a mess as he can.' He regarded the Auckland team as 'as weak as ever left the city … especially so in the backs', while the Wellington team was 'with two exceptions the same as the one that fluked Taranaki. All the old shiners were still on the roll.'

> It was one great game. The public were worked up to the high pitch of enthusiasm such as is exhibited by a principal at a hanging. Auckland tore into Wellington and Wellington tore out of the way. The Auckland forwards were too beastly rough, they shoved the home team all over the paddock. They even had the nerve to break through our scrum and race down the field with the ball. Bally cheek! … Wellington … did not attempt to score (at least that is how it appeared), but Lang kicked a goal in a moment of pique.
>
> In the second half the referee came to Wellington's assistance and gave them a try, which was converted. Thus Wellington were in front. Then to show his contempt for such a small error, Ifwerson lifted a beautiful penalty goal from wide out and Auckland had won. …

> It was exhilarating to watch the gigantic efforts of the Wellington team. One and all (excluding Pringle and Warwick) made strenuous endeavours to pull the game out of the fire, by – going for the fire brigade. ... Swain, Moffitt and Brown must have been very tired after the rest they had. You know it's hard work loafing, most fatiguing. ... Haddock commenced to shimmy every time there was a line-out. Fitzgerald was splendid till he tried to do something. Preston did put a bit of weight into the scrum, and that is to his credit. Sid Shearer once tried to execute a smart one but found his cobbers had gone to sleep. Pringle alone was a worker. His was a fine display. The backs were paralysing, so much so that they caught the complaint themselves. Warwick was the star.
>
> To the Auckland pack has to be handed the cake, and also the oven.

And so it went on.

The Southern Tour

Earlier in the month a squad of 19 players, including Nugget, had been selected to travel south and play South Canterbury on 10 September, Otago on the 13th, Southland the 17th and Canterbury the 20th. They were to depart on 8 September. On 9 September, the *Evening Post* carried a brief announcement: 'The Wellington representative team for the Southern tour left last night. There was another change in the team, J. Shearer (Poneke) replacing Pringle (Oriental) who was unable to make the trip.' Instead, Nugget was selected in a Wellington XV to play Marlborough at home the following Saturday – another match that did not make it into the scrapbook.

For the record and bearing in mind 'Tackler's criticism, the tourists beat South Canterbury 25-13. They came from behind to beat Otago 19-14, scoring four tries, lost to Southland 3-8, and were thrashed to the tune of 6-32 in Christchurch, Wellington's biggest defeat in the South Island at that time. This time it was the tourist's manager, Fred Laws, 'Tackler' was after – 'Record Breaker Fred' was the headline! Or was it a case of the Southland oysters and hospitality being responsible once again? (qv the Cornstalks)

Meanwhile …

 **Wellington v. Marlborough, 13 September 1924, Athletic Park: Playing for the B Team**

Once more we turn to 'Drop-kick', who, like 'Tackler', had been critical of the selectors for some time. This time the hosts were termed 'Wellington B', as the A team were touring the South Island. On 20 September, he wrote of the A team: '[T]here is an excuse for weaknesses, as some players could not make the trip. But there are players well worthy of a place in Wellington's A team who were available and not asked. The selectors are, no doubt, endeavouring to do their best, but their selections are causing a great deal of dissatisfaction.' And of the B's, he said, 'the Wellington team against Marlborough was a mixed one. It contained some players who ought to have been in the A team, some who deserved B team honours, and others who would have found it difficult to get a place in the junior representative team had they been playing in junior football.'

For the record, Marlborough had much the better of the play and were leading until the last 10 minutes. 'Drop-kick' again:

> The performance of the Wellington team was far from good. There was only one really good passing bout by the backs and that produced a try. The forwards did not go at all well, until in the closing stages of the game they realised that special effort was necessary to win. They managed to put an interesting finishing touch to the game. ... And though they did not win, they were lucky to avert defeat.

Thus the game ended as a 19-all draw. Of the players he wrote: '**Pringle** and **Deere** were the pick of the Wellington forwards.'

'Tackler' said much the same on 20 September, including on the subject of selection, but with a good deal less restraint – in fact, he delivered another diatribe. On the game itself, his headlines say it all: 'What! Again?'; 'Wellington Wins Half A Plum'; and 'Other Half And The Case To Marlborough'. In fact, he thought if Marlborough 'had just a quarter of the luck that went to Wellington, they would have put up a cricket score.' One cannot resist quoting his view of the Wellington backs: 'not one [of whom] would attempt to tackle decently. In this branch of the game one was reminded of the ancient nursery game of tiggy-tiggy-touchwood, a slight touch on an opponent's shoulder, and tacklers thought their duty done and expected the tackled one to get rid of the ball. But here the Wellington players made a great mistake.' He concluded that: 'Of the forwards, three stand out for special mention. Pringle was easily the best and was the shining star in the Wellington side. In fact, this player was the best on the ground. Deere and O'Regan were the only others who worked conscientiously. ... The latter kicked a magnificent goal on the call of time which robbed Marlborough of a win.'

**Wellington v. King Country,
20 September 1924, Athletic Park:
'Tackler's Third Lamentation**

The last cutting of a match report in the scrapbook is by 'Tackler' and is dated 27 September 1924. As such, and as it deals also with Wellington's season overall, it is only fair that we should give 'Tackler' his head as he rails against all and sundry.

**FITTING FINALE
WELLINGTON'S WOOP WOOP REPS
'KANNED' BY KING COUNTRY**

The King Country came down, and with a complete lack of combination and science, ripped a hole in the Wellington defence big enough to push a battleship through. … Soon after commencement it was easily guessed that another of the awful displays so prevalent this season was to be staged, and it was not long before the truth was brought home. It devolved into a burlesque, and such cries as 'Give us a bob's worth' and 'A team of schoolboys would lick you' were thrown out to the players by the disgusted spectators. The team underwent one or two changes, but, unfortunately, for the worst.

> Their putrid showing was not the result of King Country being such a wonderful combination. They were anything but that, but one thing they did do was to attempt to give the public something for their money. Their forwards were quite good, lacking some of the finer points of the game, but their backs were wretched. Wellington's were worse. … The only redeeming factor about the Wellington van was that they hooked the ball nine-tenths of the game, but this proved to be rather a disadvantage, for when the backs got it, they made a terrible hash of things. … There was not a player who used his brains.
>
> The final score of 18 points to 12 easily represents the merits of the two teams. King Country can owe their victory to the forwards, who played remarkably well. … Not much can be said regarding the [Wellington] forwards except that Pringle played his usual game, which certainly throws no discredit on him.

Having dealt with the match itself, 'Tackler' turned his attention to the state of rugby in the Capital:

> If ever the football following public have had a sickener of the game they have had it this year … not once have they been rewarded with a decent game. By reversing the old phrase "They came to scoff and remained to pray" one gets about the feeling of those unfortunates who have been asked to dub up the nimble shilling each Saturday. On the exhibitions given the public should have been paid a dollar a head for attending. This downward trend in the standard of our play is alarming.

He demanded a change of selectors: 'Everybody is disgusted with their work – the public, the players, and perhaps the Rugby Union itself.' Once again he warned of the threat of League drawing on Union players and the crowds: 'And do not forget that is the way the ship is heading at the present juncture.' He mooted the possibility of a sole selector replacing the triumvirate, as was the case with Auckland and the very successful Hawke's Bay side, and concluded: 'The future of Wellington football is at stake, and the onus is on the clubs to see that next season is not a repetition of this year's sorry selection.'

A Final Word on Nugget's 1924

The man had given body and soul to the game he obviously loved. He had played his heart out competing for a berth with the Invincibles, and having missed out so narrowly there, continued to play his heart out for club and province. He may have lost a bit of fire, and his form may have dropped a little at one time, but by the end of the season he was still, more often than not, as good as any other player on the field. He had been unlucky to miss out on a second cap in 1923. He had been extremely unlucky to miss out on the northern tour Home. He turned 25 at the end of the year and had several years of football ahead of him. What more did Dame Fortune hold in store?

CHAPTER 9
1925 Annus Horribilis

Autumn 1925 saw the New Zealand public looking forward to another All Black tour of New South Wales. They were to play eight matches, beginning and ending in Wellington, against Wellington on 3 June and Wellington-Manawatu-Horowhenua on 8 July. Their six intervening games in Australia would include three 'tests'. The team was to be made up of players who had not travelled with the Invincibles. There was also to be a return match with NSW in Auckland on 19 September.

According to 'Racket' ('Rapid Rise in Rugby', 1939),

before the first game of the season W.F. Hornig [president of the NZRU and also president of the Oriental Club] approached 'Nugget' in the dressing shed and asked if he would be available for the tour of Australia, adding '"Nugget', you're in the team". … The match that day was between Oriental and University at Lyall Bay, and in the second spell, while defending the northern goal, Pringle suffered a broken leg from a heavy tackle.

From the archives, we learn that this account of his injury was, in essence, correct, but it was not the first game of the season, and Nugget's run of ill-fortune was a little worse and more complicated than that.

According to the *Evening Post* of 20 April 1925, Oriental's season opener was a 16-38 defeat at the hands of Poneke on 18 April. 'A notable absentee for Oriental was Pringle, who is reported to be suffering from appendicitis.' This was confirmed in the 25 April edition of *NZ Truth*: 'Nugget Pringle, the Oriental, Wellington and New Zealand forward fell victim to appendicitis last week. The big fellow is stiff – he just missed the English trip and now the Sydney trip is gone.' But the *Post* of 24 April had more up-to-date news: 'It is pleasing to record that the report that "Nugget" Pringle was suffering from appendicitis is incorrect. The tall Oriental forward is likely to be with the team in the next game. He had enough bad luck last year, and the hope is that there may be no more coming his way.'

But, sadly, such was to be the case. There being no rugby on the intervening Anzac weekend, the next game was on 2 May against Petone, which Oriental lost 18-0. Nugget was in the team according to the *Post* of 4 May, and 'at one stage, had a very good chance of doing something to assist his side, but he found difficulty in handling the greasy ball'; while later: 'From the kick-off in the second spell Pringle marked and sent the ball well down field.' All to no avail.

Now came the Varsity game at Lyall Bay on 9 May. From the *Post* of 11 May we learn that this was a close and exciting game, the lead changing hands several times. Late in the game, Varsity levelled the score at 16-16 when Martin-Smith scored a try and O'Regan kicked a poster. The crowd would have been well content to leave it at that, but not so Varsity. Ories were fighting with their backs to the wall, Pringle having gone off and leaving only 14 men. 'Varsity drove home the general offensive, and Sceats scored' the winning try, the game ending at 19-16 to Varsity. Elsewhere in the same report it was confirmed that Nugget had gone off with a leg injury.

Finally, from our old friend 'Tackler', this from 6 June:

> Present at Athletic Park, Wellington, last Saturday, was friend Nugget Pringle, on crutches. It will be some time before the big fellow is seen in action again, perhaps not until next season. Nug. is the stiffest of stiff players. He only missed the Home trip by a whisker, and had he not broken a bone in a leg he would have been on his way to Sydney by now.

And, indeed, it does seem that Nugget was out for the season.

'Racket' ('Rapid Rise in Rugby', 1939) again: 'The same year "Nugget" was operated on for a broken nose sustained the previous season, and to cap the year off of ill-luck he was operated on for appendicitis.' Nugget himself confirmed this when he enlisted for the Army in 1941. He included in his past medical history a broken nose in 1923, and surgery to his nose and on his appendix in 1925. Presumably his appendicitis had recurred or grumbled on. He did not mention the broken leg – the form inquired about joint injuries but not broken limbs!

CHAPTER 10

1926 Back in Action:
In Search of Form and Fitness

Despite Nugget's tribulations in 1925, '[h]is enthusiasm for the game could not be quenched, and he was out again for Oriental in 1926, taking part in all the home matches for Wellington that year' ('Racket', 'Rapid Rise in Rugby', 1939). Which, in truth, was not quite the case.

In 1926 *NZ Truth* came out on Thursdays instead of Saturdays, and the rugby reports were more diffuse with less of Wellington. The 'Our National Field Game' column no longer appeared, and what was written does not have the smack of our old friend 'Tackler' about it. For that reason, the information contained in the account below was culled from the *Evening Post* archives unless otherwise stated.

Again, there was to be an All Black tour of New South Wales, commencing once again with a pipe-opener against Wellington on 30 June. One would have thought that this did not give Nugget time to regain fitness and form sufficient to be in the frame for All Black selection. He played in the first game of the season on 24 April – a 5-14 defeat at the hands of Petone, when once again 'Pringle, Sly and Moffitt were Oriental's leading forwards', but did not feature in the report of the thrashing of

Wellington by Oriental a week later and did not play when they trounced Poneke 17-0 the following week. However, he was back on the field to score a try in the six-try victory over Selwyn on 15 May. All games were called off the following Saturday because of Wellington weather.

Nugget continued to turn out for Oriental, playing in the loss to Athletic on 29 May – the same day on which another Pringle, presumably his 18-year-old brother Frank, scored a try and kicked a conversion in Ories' third division defeat of Onslow. By the end of May, Nugget's name, according to one report, had been put forward for consideration for the North Island team, the inter-island game being listed for Athletic Park on 12 June.

Meanwhile, on 27 May it was reported that he had been selected 'to represent Wellington in a special match with Canterbury, at Christchurch, on 3rd June'. He did not get a mention in the match report, but there is no reason to doubt that he played. In the event, the game was lost 12-13. By all accounts Canterbury were lucky. Mark Nicholls, who otherwise played well, had left his kicking boots on the ferry.

Two days later Nugget was back home to score a try in the 8-4 defeat of Marist on 5 June. 'NZ *Truth*'s Special Wellington Representative' opined on 3 June: 'Pringle is not back to last year's form and his inclusion in the first rep. game came as a surprise. However, at his best Pringle is a solid forward.' It was reported in the same issue that he was not among Wellington's ten official nominations for the North Island team. In the event, neither he nor Big Jim made the side, although H. Sly, Oriental's captain, was a reserve – and, for completeness, it was a record 41-9 win to the Northerners.

After the inter-island game, the selectors announced the names of the 23 players to tour Australia. Nugget's was not among them. There were 13 of the Invincibles, another five who had toured Australia in 1925, and only five new caps.

There followed a bye for the Ories, followed by, on 26 June, a 0-0 draw with Berhampore, in which 'Moffit, Sly and Pringle caught the eye in the Oriental vanguard'. This was in preparation for what, four days later, was one of the bigger games of the season – one in which Nugget and Big Jim might show the selectors a thing or two.

WELLINGTON V. NEW ZEALAND,
Wednesday, 30 June 1926,
Athletic Park

> General opinion being that the team for Australia is one of the finest Rugby combinations ever selected to represent the Dominion, it was not expected that the tourists would be seriously troubled by a Wellington team, minus the services of Porter, M. Nicholls and Svenson [who were with the opposition! Of the original selection, H.E. Nicholls, Fitzgerald and Warden had dropped out also]. The match was of greater importance to Wellington than to New Zealand, for it served as a splendid trial for the selection of the team to meet Hawkes Bay [in the forthcoming Ranfurly Shield challenge]. (*Evening Post*, 1 July 1926)

The weather was 'bleak and damp', with a biting southerly and a greasy ball, and hence a relatively small crowd. The teams were as follows:

NEW ZEALAND

Stevenson
Elvy, Blake, Robilliard
Svenson, Sheen
Mill
Porter (captain)
Kirkpatrick, Lomas, C. Brownlie, Harvey, Finlayson,
Hazlett, Knight

WELLINGTON

Malcolm
Tait, Grenfell, Malfroy
McKenzie, Corner
Bramwell
Jessup
Wilson, O'Regan, Pringle, Moffitt (captain), Thomas,
Tyree, Taylor

The toss favoured New Zealand who played with the wind ... the Dominion representatives worked down, and ... Elvy was sent in a dash for the line [and was] brought down. [From a scrum the Wellington forwards cleared.'The Blacks' came again:] Porter was heading well for a try, when **Malfroy** came across to force in the nick of time ... Wellington made a hot reply ... from a scrum, **Tyree** broke away and dived over. **Malcolm's** kick missed by inches.

>Wellington ... 3
>New Zealand ... 0

[Play swung back and forth, **Malcolm** missed] a chance to goal. ... In riposte, also from a free-kick, Svenson, with splendid judgement, landed a goal, though not before the ball had struck the cross-bar.

>Wellington ... 3
>New Zealand ... 3

[Sheen, injured, was replaced by Dalley at half-back, Mill moving to first five. When] **Malcolm** failed to find the line with a relieving kick, the tourists got busy. ... The ball was sent out to Elvy, [who scored with] a brilliant dash. [Svenson converted.]

>Wellington ... 3
>New Zealand ... 8

[After more] vigorous forward work by the home team, [the New Zealand backs took over and were] seen to perfection. ... The ball travelled through the line to Elvy, who finished off with a try. Svenson failed to goal.

Wellington ... 3
New Zealand ... 11

The touring side was now playing like a winning team, [but failed to score again before half-time.]

[In the second spell,] Svenson did not come out. Porter took the second five-eighths position, C. Brownlie played as wing-forward, and Alley filled the gap in the pack. Immediately after the interval **Moffitt** headed a strong Wellington rush, to which the Blacks made reply. In the subsequent play, however, the Wellington forwards hustled the opposition, whose task was made heavier by a slightly-increased wind. [Ultimately,] New Zealand was penalised, **Malcolm** making sure of a goal.

Wellington ... 6
New Zealand ... 11

Wellington were still able to gain an advantage in loose play. [Following] a dribbling rush [and] a scramble, **Bramwell** whipped the leather out to **Corner**, who in turn passed to **McKenzie**. **Grenfell** was next to receive [and touched down] behind the posts. **Malcolm's** kick was poor. [And, indeed, it must have been, to miss from that position!]

Wellington ... 9
New Zealand ... 11

The game was now in Wellington's favour. Rush after rush kept the tourists busy on the defensive. The local backs were rendering good assistance to the keen battling forwards, but through misjudged kicks some opportunities were lost. The chance for the lead came when Hazlett was caught off-side, and **O'Regan** made no mistake with the kick. [**Malcolm** appears to have been given the sack – or boot!]

Wellington ... 12
New Zealand ... 11

Stirred to greater effort, New Zealand, per medium of Mill, Porter, Finlayson and C. Brownlie looked like regaining the lead when a pass forward held up the advance. Forwards and backs were striving hard, but Wellington kept a strict eye on all movements, and driving the Blacks back, improved their position [with a free kick by **O'Regan**.]

Wellington ... 15
New Zealand ... 11

For some time the local team carried on its aggressive policy in fine style, forwards and backs playing up splendidly. [Harvey was caught off-side, and it was **O'Regan's** turn to kick a goal off the cross-bar.]

> Wellington ... 18
> New Zealand ... 11

A little later the Wellington backs were seen in a fine bout which cleared the defence and left enough room for **Tait** to dash across near the corner. **O'Regan's** kick was a trifle short.

> Wellington ... 21
> New Zealand ... 11

In the closing stages New Zealand showed their superiority, but their efforts, mainly of the open order, were too late. ... Just on the call of time Porter and Elvy cleared the way for a dash by Finlayson. The big forward galloped off from the vicinity of half-way, and although grounded by **Bramwell**, who went for Finlayson's ankles, he had enough weight to slide over the Wellington line. Porter just failed to goal. [What a try! 'Bunny' Finlayson from Maungaturoto was 6'2" and weighed 15 stone! And so the game ended, with the final score:]

> Wellington ... 21
> New Zealand ... 14

The journalist who penned the match report thought, while noting that some of the principals of the New Zealand team were absent, resting or recovering from injury, others were out of position, and there was concern of 'the risk of possible injury, … Wellington must be given credit for a splendid performance, equally as pleasing as that in the match with Canterbury a few weeks ago.'

The *Evening Post* reviewed the match again on 3 July and thought 'the chances of getting a really good team together for the Shield match are much improved. … Moffitt … has no equal as a lock. … Tyree was always in the picture, and Pringle was a "star" in line-out work.' *NZ Truth* of 8 July concurred:

> Playing as if life was at stake, the Wellingtonians – looking much too light for the pick of New Zealand – made every post a winning one; never at any stage did they let up and never looked like being beaten. … The outcome of this victory will mean greater confidence for the selectors in selecting a team to try conclusions with Hawkes Bay for the Ranfurly Shield on August 14. [And of the forwards:] Moffitt will – barring accidents – retain his place at lock. … Tyree, on present form, is assured of a position in the pack, as also are Thomas and Pringle.

On 22 July, reviewing the latest club games, *NZ Truth* said: 'Jim Moffitt has a lien on the lock possy for the rep. games and Pringle is recognised as one not to be dispensed with for the line-outs.' And, indeed, Moffitt, Tyree and Pringle retained their places in the Wellington XV announced on 19 July for the next representative game.

Wellington v. New Zealand Maoris, 21 July 1926, Athletic Park

This was the last game for the Maoris on a short New Zealand tour. Two days later they would sail for Sydney *en route* for France and the United Kingdom. George Nepia withdrew from the match a day or two beforehand. The teams were:

NEW ZEALAND MAORIS

Potaka
Falwasser, Barclay, Phillips
Kingi, Bell
Shortland
Haupapa, Olsen, Stewart, Matene, Manihera, Rika, S. Gemmell, Wilson

WELLINGTON

Taylor
Tait, South, Sutton
Corner, Mackenzie
H.E. Nicholls
Jessup
O'Regan, Warden, Pringle, Moffitt, Tyree, A.L. Thomas, Taylor

Conditions were good, 'the southerly wind presenting little hindrance. ... Before the ball was set in motion, the tourists gave a haka, which was appreciated by some five thousand spectators.' It was a 'fast and open game', but the Maoris, like the All Blacks before them, suffered from lack of preparation as well as 'the fact that the doubt about the tour had caused no little anxiety'. Nonetheless, Wellington were superior in all departments, and won handsomely, to the tune of 28-16. The Maoris' 'dash … came in bursts', and they 'were inclined to lob their passes'. Their greatest success came in 'breaking away from … loose scrambles. These bursts were often spectacular, and while they accounted for some measure of success the portion of the Maoris would have been greater had those breaking away been accorded more support.'

Insofar as the run of play went, with the scores level at 3-3, 'the forwards came to light with a splendid passing rush. **Tyree** started off from a line-out, **Moffitt** carried on, **Warden** took a hand, and finally **Pringle** dodged an opponent and finished off a great piece of play. **O'Regan** was not permitted to take the kick.' Curious. No reason was given.

Nugget had now played, and won, for and against the All Blacks, and against New Zealand Maoris, scoring tries in two of the three games. Some record!

The *NZ Truth* of 29 July, reviewing the Maoris game, opined: 'Pringle was the best forward on the ground. He should be away with the All Blacks. Lofty is playing better than ever in his life.' Unfortunately for Lofty, there would be no more All Black caps on offer for almost two years.

Three days after the Maoris game, Nugget was back on the field for Oriental's loss to Varsity, and again when they thrashed Petone a week later, while in the same week his selection was announced for the Wellington squad to play Hawkes Bay in the Shield challenge on 14 August. *NZ Truth* of 5 August thought that as flankers, 'Pringle and Barry would balance well and both are in great form'. Nugget could now look forward to the final games of the club championship and a lengthy representative season including a southern tour. In the event, Dame Fortune had other ideas.

The Oriental v. Athletic match on 7 August, as reported in the *Evening Post* of 9 August 1926 contained the following: 'Pringle, the Oriental forward, was injured in the first spell and was replaced by Butters.' *NZ Truth* of 12 August said: 'Very genuine regret from all sides was expressed that Pringle had to leave the field. During his short sojourn on the ground he displayed some of his old form, and it was a terrible pity an unfortunate accident should happen along, just on the eve of Wellington's most important fixture. From all accounts it is pretty certain Pringle will not do the Bay trip.'

The *Evening Post* on 10 August was more optimistic: 'Pringle, who was injured last Saturday, is able to make the trip.' However, he was not in the team which lost to Wairarapa the following day, and on 13 August, the eve of the Challenge, it was reported that: 'Pringle has not recovered sufficiently from the injury received last Saturday, and the absence of this tall forward, particularly in the line-out, will be keenly felt by Wellington.'

Nugget did not play again that season, neither in Ories' last two games (they finished third), nor in any of the remaining nine representative fixtures. He was not selected for the southern tour and did not play even on those occasions when two Wellington teams were playing, home and away, on the same day. Given the weakness of some of these sides, this cannot have been because of lack of form. One can but conclude that the (unspecified) injury was more serious than first thought, or that some intercurrent condition supervened.

The Shield Challenge was a debacle, lost 58-8, as the Bay team, with ten All Blacks including the Brownlies, ran into, through and over the challengers who were completely demoralised after the first 20 minutes. The legality of their methods was questioned by elements of the Wellington press, with the suggestion that the referee was unduly lenient. Ultimately it was deemed that 'all's fair in love and war', and the Bay proved their point in the return match at the end of the season, when, lacking ten key players, they still defeated Wellington (although with only six who had played in the Challenge) comfortably, and with a 'home' referee.

After the Maoris game, Wellington contrived to lose nine games, including all on the southern tour, some by quite big margins, in exchange for narrow wins away at Nelson and at home over the Seddon Shield Districts. In the final report of the season, 'After the Ball', *NZ Truth*'s Special Wellington Representative concluded lamely: 'The season has ended and from the point of view of victories it has been one of Wellington's worst. Still *NZ Truth* is inclined to the view that our football is going to be better in the future.' One could not but hope so. Oh, 'Tackler', how we miss your passion and your prose!

CHAPTER 11

1927 Another Crack of the Whip – With a Broken Arm

Once again Nugget was starting from scratch after a long lay-off. He had recovered sufficiently from whatever had ailed him in the spring to turn out once more for Pastimes in the Mercantile League in the early summer of a season in which they went on to win the League. Before Christmas his name featured in match reports most Mondays, usually with runs, occasionally with wickets. That was until 10 January; from that date his name did not reappear before the end of the season. The likely explanation was provided by 'Drop-kick' in the *Evening Post* of 9 April 1927, as he reviewed club prospects for the forthcoming rugby championship. Of Oriental he wrote: 'Pringle, who broke an arm recently, may not be ready for the start of the season.' The how, why and where of this injury we know not. We do know that he was now on the management committee of the club.

Meanwhile, thoughts turned to the forthcoming representative season. With no All Black fixtures in 1927, the eagerly anticipated 1928 tour of South Africa loomed large, and four trial games were proposed, including one involving a combined Wellington side, and one being the North-South match on 3 September – a similar programme to that employed in 1924 for selection of the Invincibles.

At the same time, the Wellington Union, after several disappointing seasons and much debate, replaced their selectorial triumvirate with one man – Southland-born Otago graduate and Wellington schoolmaster, John Norman Millard, christened by *NZ Truth* the 'First Professor of Rugby'. Only six representative fixtures were on the programme, and a section of the press favoured this, believing the limited number would give the team time and opportunity to build.

Although 'Drop-kick' reported in the *Post* at the end of April that Pringle was 'now practically right' to return to the fray, he did not do so until 28 May against Petone. The game was played in bright sunshine on 'very treacherous ground', and *NZ Truth* on 2 June noted that: 'Pringle made his reappearance for Oriental, but he was far from being ready.' Wellington's first game of the season (Taranaki at Hawera, as usual) was only five weeks away. Much work to be done, one might have thought.

'Drop-kick', however, saw the Petone game through different lenses, writing in the *Post* on 4 June that: 'Pringle was a tower of strength among the Oriental forwards, and was always a source of danger to Petone. Besides putting a lot of useful weight into the scrums he was a dominating figure in the line-outs and was always prominent in the loose.' And it seems 'Drop-kick' may have been the better judge, for Nugget stood out week in, week out, for the next month. On 24 June, after a loss to Varsity in a biting southerly and heavy rain, he reported 'Pringle is rapidly regaining his form of two years ago', while *NZ Truth* on 7 July, writing of the loss to Athletic five days earlier, thought 'Lofty Pringle was outstanding amongst the forwards of the defeated side'.

Going largely for the 'old guard', and certainly on his form, 'Professor' Millard included Nugget in the team for the Taranaki fixture.

Wellington v. Taranaki, 6 July 1927, Hawera

On the day following the match the *Evening Post* told of a close game with Wellington ultimately coming out on top, five tries to three. Nugget played a prominent part in forward rushes leading to two tries in the first half, while towards the close: 'The final score came from a scramble, from which **Kilby** picked up, handed to **McHardy**, the latter giving **Pringle** a short pass. **Nicholls** failed in his attempt to goal.' Final score: Wellington 15, Taranaki 11.

NZ Truth, reviewing the match, had this to say on 14 July: 'The best forward on the ground was Pringle. The writer has never seen the big fellow play better.' In the same issue, in a review of the Poneke game played three days later, we read: 'Pringle continued in the good form he displayed against Taranaki and on Saturday he was the best forward participating.'

Not a bad month's work after a nine-month lay-off with injuries. However, Footballing Fate's fickle fingers were furtling in his pie once more, and he did not play again in July. He was selected for the game against South Canterbury on 27 July, but withdrew a few days beforehand, through injury, and next turned out for his club on 6 August. Once again he found form, and was chosen for the next rep. match.

 Wellington v. Southland, 17 August 1927, Athletic Park

A comfortable win for the home side, 21-9, in which 'Pringle found a way over in the corner' for the final score of the game.

'Drop-kick' in the *Post* wrote: 'Pringle shone out in the line-outs and went very well in the second half with Edgar in support', while *NZ Truth*, 25 August, thought 'Pringle was outstanding in the forwards and has clearly returned to the form that got him into the All Black trials and within an ace of the 1924 trip'. Three days later, against Berhampore, he 'played a fine game among the forwards. He received a knock in the second half, but carried on and was a great asset to the team'. Having scored against Southland, Nugget was now in try-scoring mood, picking up another in that game, and a third for Wellington against Manawhenua a week later.

One cannot but pause at this point to admire the man's resilience. The manner in which he rediscovered his best form so quickly, time and again, after injury, this in days when intensive rehabilitation had not been dreamt of, speaks volumes not only for his skills, but also for his fitness, determination and dedication.

 Wellington v. Manawhenua, 27 August 1927, Athletic Park

Although at the time the visitors held the Ranfurly Shield, it was not at stake, this being for them an away game. Nonetheless, they were soundly beaten, 23-14, in ideal conditions 'except for a keen southerly wind', and in front of 'fully ten thousand spectators'. With the score at 3-0 and '[a]fter some give-and-take play **Johnson** made a break and passed to **Pringle,** who worked his way across for a try, which **Malcolm** converted with a splendid kick', making the score 8-0. Once again, according to the 1 September *NZ Truth*: 'Pringle, the tall man of the team, shone in the line-outs. "Lofty" uses his head well, one time passing out to the backs and the next putting the ball at toe and coming through.'

**Wellington v. Otago,
3 September 1927, Athletic Park**

Wellington won the match 24-16 — their fifth win on the trot — with the game being described by the *Evening Post* of 3 September as 'fast and open [before] fully eleven thousand spectators.' The *Post* observed: 'Wellington were well-served in the matter of generalship, the experience of eight New Zealand representatives counting for a great deal [and] Wellington deserved the win, for which they had to give their best performance to date.' Of Nugget, the *NZ Truth* of 8 September had this to say:

> Pringle made a bird of sending back to Kilby and the brilliant little half always did the correct thing by sending on to Johnson. ... Pringle was one of the best forwards on the ground. When on his game — and 'Lofty' was right there in this match — there are few who can give him points in the line-out work. He made a feature of this, and Wellington backs can thank 'Lofty' for providing most of their opportunities to open up the play.

For the record, this was the Wellington line-up Otago faced (All Blacks in italics):

Malcolm
Elvy, South, *Svenson*
Johnson, M. *Nicholls*
Kilby[1]
Porter
O'Regan, Claridge, *Pringle*, Emerson
Taylor, S. *Shearer*, L.A. *Thomas*

 **Wellington v. Canterbury,
10 September 1927, Athletic Park**

A week later Wellington faced Canterbury, now the Shield-holders, but again the Shield was not at stake. Of the team that played Otago, Elvy and Malcolm were out. The conditions were 'all that could be desired', the crowd close on 18,000, and before the match the teams lined up and gave three hearty cheers for the watching Governor General, His Excellency Sir Charles Fergusson. The game itself was described as 'fast and stirring', even 'exhilarating', as Wellington led all the way to win 20-17. *NZ Truth* of 15 September noted: 'Pringle had some half-nelsons applied to him in the line-outs. He generally went down with two or three men hanging on, but before falling he nearly always got the ball back to Kilby.'

---

1   Frank Kilby was capped the following year, when he toured South Africa, and went on to an illustrious career as player and captain, and later, administrator and manager, including of Wilson Whineray's 1963–64 side which toured Britain and France with such success.

Wellington v. Auckland, 17 September 1927, Eden Park

Next up was an away game against Auckland, also undefeated to date. Wellington were without Porter, Svenson and Elvy. The conditions were 'atrocious', windy, with 'teeming rain', and the ground 'treacherous ... churned up by curtain-raisers ... a large part of the playing area a sea of mud', as before 13,000 people Wellington were hammered to the tune of 21-3. In their defence, Wellington played into the worst of the storm in the second half, while their previous victories had been at home in good conditions, and here their star-studded backline was doused by the Auckland weather. According to the *Evening Post* of 19 September: 'Outstanding among the Wellington forwards were Oliver and Pringle, the former going extremely well in the loose. Pringle also showed dash and was conspicuous for work on the line-out, though hampered by tactics which should have brought more penalties than they did.' While *NZ Truth* of 22 September thought:

> Pringle was undoubtedly the outstanding forward in the visiting team. His great reach in the line-out was effective – for a while – but his bustling methods carried him right through the game as a danger to be watched. He is a handy man in any team. Emerson used his weight effectively and coupled up with Pringle often in some fine loose rushing stunts.

On Trial for South Africa

The representative season was all but over, and a series of trials similar to those played in 1924 to select the Invincibles were underway. There would be regional matches, Possibles-Probables and inter-island games, and a final Possibles-Probables contest. There is no doubt that Nugget's name was in the mix – 'Drop-kick', who described his performance against Auckland as 'outstanding' included his name among those 'who appear to be well in the running for places' on 24 September after the first Trial fixture.

Wellington-Manawhenua v. Taranaki-Wanganui, 21 September 1927, Spriggens Park, Wanganui

Played in ideal conditions, the first trial involving Nugget was won by the Wellington combined team, and to be fair, the *Evening Post* of 22 September reported that: 'Reviewing the game of the individual players, it must be said that few impressed as being of All Black class.' However, it went on to say 'of the Wellington-Manawhenua forwards, Pringle, Galpin, Olliver and Taylor were the most prominent. Pringle's reach in the line-outs was of great assistance.' Indeed, the first try came when 'Pringle's long reach took the ball in the line-out, transferred to Johnson, who passed to South, who ran in to score under the posts'.

'Changes were made in the teams for the second session', when 'Thomas replaced Pringle'. The *Post* thought that: 'The fact Pringle was not required to play in the second half may be taken as an indication that the tall Wellington forward satisfied the selectors by his performance in the first spell.' It may have been a planned substitution, but it could well be that Nugget, in addition, had taken a knock, as he was not in the team for Wellington's final game of the season against Wairarapa three days later, when others who had played in the trial were.

NZ Truth of 29 September, reviewing the trial, judged that, of the side-rowers, Ward and Pringle 'should have gained favour with the selectors. Ward was really the best forward on the ground. … Pringle was a master in the line-out work and when it came to quick following-up, Lofty was always on hand. He is an unfortunate player and it would be just his luck to receive an injury that would spoil his chances.' However, again to be fair, the writer concluded by naming Ward but not Nugget as likely to 'gain favour with the selectors'.

And *NZ Truth* was spot on. On 25 September the selectors announced the teams for the North Island Possibles-Probables match to be played two days later. The side rows were the Brownlies and Finlayson, incumbents from previous All Black tours, together with Ward. Having missed out on selection for that match, Nugget missed out on the inter-island fixture on 1 October also.

Without him in the line-out, but in his place Maurice Brownlie and Finlayson on the sides and Cyril Brownlie and McWilliams at the back, the North team, the bookies' favourites, lost a thriller 30-31. Following the game the selectors announced 13 certainties for the tour, together with the teams for the final Possibles-Probables trial to be played on 5 October, contesting the other 16 places. The loose forwards among the certainties included the aforementioned incumbents, together with two All Blacks from the South Island, Ron Stewart and Bill Hazlett, a member of the team defeated by Wellington the previous year. Not among the certainties, Nugget was named among the 'emergencies' for both teams for the final trial, and, judging by the match report, his services were not required.

The same evening the selectors, as was their practice, announced the names of the complementary 16 for South Africa.

Nugget's name was not among them. Ward and McWilliams got the nod. In general, the selectors were lauded for picking a very strong side, and there was no serious criticism from the press, including 'Drop-kick', who wrote in the *Post*:

> The forwards as a body cannot be faulted. Still, going back through the trials, it is evident that not a few players equal in rank to some of the elect have been passed over. With the wealth of material it was to be expected that some of the fine forwards would be unlucky. In the list of rejected players there is A. Pringle, whose turn for a taste of good fortune is long over-due. He has few equals in line-out play.

A fitting epitaph for Nugget's 1927 season.

> Whatever disappointment or anger he felt at his omission, he dispelled later that month on the cricket pitch. Playing once more for Pastimes, he scored 24 and took 6 for 7 against Samuels and Kelly on 15 October, 20 not out and 2 for 20 against Education A on 22 October, and 42 against Shipping on 29 October. He ended his year with two wickets for no runs against Hyams on 5 December.

CHAPTER 12

1928 and 1929 Brother Frank – And a Kick in the Teeth

Now 28 years old, Nugget hung up his football boots at the beginning of the year, and with them, very probably, his cricket boots, we know not why. Pastimes played in the 'A' Grade of the Mercantile League. The scores from the previous Saturday's cricket were published in Monday's *Evening Post*. Those of the Mercantile League were brief, incomplete and occasionally missing. Nonetheless, over the years, Nugget was credited with runs or wickets most weeks. The fact that his name did not appear for the remainder of the 1927–28 season after 5 December can be taken as strong evidence that he was not playing.

As for football, the name Pringle did appear in the Oriental line-up regularly from the beginning of the 1928 season, initially for the Senior B's, later promoted to the A's, but it was that of his younger brother Frank. Now 20 years of age, Frank had worked his way up from the Thirds, through the Juniors, to the B's over the previous two years, and, in addition to scoring a few tries, was the regular goal-kicker.

With the A's top of the table, 'Drop-kick' wrote on 23 June: 'Although A. Pringle, the ex-New Zealand representative and a player who has had more than his share of bad luck, is not taking the field for Oriental this season, he is doing a great deal of hard work in the interest of the team. No little credit is due to him for the senior A team's showing to date.'

But fate had another twist in store. As the season progressed further, the A's challenge fizzled out, and University went on to claim both the Championship and the Cup, with Poneke as runners-up. Meanwhile the B's reached the semi-finals of the Knock-Out Cup, where they were drawn to play Hutt on 11 August. According to 'Racket', writing of Nugget in 1939:

[H]is last game of rugby was played for the Oriental senior B team in 1928, Nugget being asked to play to combat W. Peck, a good line-out forward with Hutt. Breaking away from a scrum with the ball at toe, he endeavoured to kick the ball but caught the Hutt half-back in the mouth, the unfortunate Hutt player suffering numerous fractures of the jaw. This decided the big fellow to end his Rugby career, but for several years subsequently he was a member of the committee of the Oriental club. ('Racket', 'Rapid Rise in Rugby', 1939)

The *Evening Post* confirms the details of the game itself. The Oriental team listed on 9 August included 'Pringle 2' (i.e., Alex and Frank), and the Hutt line-up 'Peck'. According to the Monday edition, Oriental won 9-0, but there is no match report and no mention is made of the half-back's injury. This appears to have been the only occasion on which the two brothers played in the same XV. The final was played against Johnsonville, the B grade champions, on 8 September. There were seven changes in the Oriental team which included neither brother. Without the crisp support of the Pringles, the B's lost 14-6. However, there is a twist to this tale, as there was a re-match with Hutt (now Lower Hutt) almost exactly 12 months later (see below).

> The 1928 season over, Nugget dusted off his cricket boots once more, and in the first reported Pastimes fixture took 6 for 10 against Picot's on 3 November, followed by 5 Odlin's wickets for 43 in the New Year.

On 13 April 1929 'Drop-kick' took a look at the new club season, and of Oriental wrote:

> A. Pringle, the ex-New Zealand representative forward, who had quite a run of bad luck, is apparently standing down again this season, although he will no doubt be assisting the coach in looking after the players, as he did last season. [Others] and [Frank] Pringle (brother of the former representative) are among last year's forwards in the running for places in Oriental's senior team.

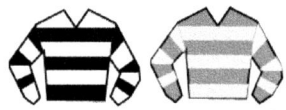

Nonetheless, Nugget took the field one more time. The *Evening Post* of 5 August 1929 carries a report of 'the game between Lower Hutt and Oriental, which virtually decided the Senior B championship. ... Pringle, the ex-All Black, turned out for Oriental.' The game was played on 3 August. The previous evening paper carried the teams. Both Pringles were down to play, but in the event only Nugget was in the XV on the day. Peck played once more for Lower Hutt, whose half-back was

Gordon. The *Hutt News* of 8 August 1929 goes into more detail of the game, which Hutt won 12-3. Of Nugget it reports:

> Peck sustained his form in the line-out work and shared the honours with Nugget Pringle in this department. Baker had the job of looking after Pringle and did his work thoroughly. … Nugget Pringle played a surprisingly good game for 'Ories'. His habit of throwing the ball back in the line-out was of little use to his side, as the Hutt forwards had been instructed to break through on the opposing backs.

And of the Hutt half-back: '[In the second half,] Gordon received a kick on the mouth, which necessitated his leaving the field. … "Rats" Gordon received rather a painful injury, quite a number of his front teeth being broken off. It was purely an accident and no one was more concerned than the man responsible.'

So there we have it. It is highly probable that this was Nugget's last game – the game in which he occasioned injury to the opposing half-back, and the game he described to 'Racket'. A sad and ironic end to the career of such a clean player.

Fig.28. North Island representatives 1924. Framed photograph with 'Mrs Pringle' handwritten on back. Back Row – I.H.Harvey, L Knight, C.Brownlie, J.A.McNab, C.Porter. Standing – Q Donald, M.Brownlie, A.Pringle, A.West, A.R.Lomas, W.R.Irvine. Second Row – G.Nepia, H.W.Brown, A.H.Hart, H.Murphy (manager), F.W.Lucas, L.Paewai, J.Mills, K.Svensen. In Front – H.E.Nicholls, M.Nicholls, B.Cooke. (New Zealand Rugby Museum, courtesy of Stephen Berg.)

Fig.29. Nugget's nuptials (1934), with his bride Janet (Jean), flanked by brother Frank and his bride-to-be Cicely, the author's mother.

Fig.30. Officiating at the athletics. Originally published in the Free Lance, 9 March 1943.

Fig.31. In uniform, Christchurch, 1945.

Fig.32. Nugget and Jean at home in Christchurch.

Fig.33. Captioned by Nugget 'With Bob Paton, Old-Timers Day.' An Evening Post press photograph of 10 October 1952. Bob Paton is almost certainly Robert James Paton, previously a Buller and Wellington rep., and a senior referee in Nugget's playing years. He was the brother of Harry Paton, Otago and Wellington rep., also a referee, and All Black #148.

Fig.34. Nugget's jersey (courtesy of the Oriental Rongotai Football Club).

Fig.35. Nugget's Wellington cap.

Fig.36. His All Black cap.

CHAPTER 13

The 1930s, the War Years and Illness Strikes

On a day in 1934 Nugget stood at the altar, brother Frank beside him as best man. His bride was Janet Turnbull Maguire, nee Turnbull Weir, and they were to enjoy almost 40 years together, the marriage ending with her death in 1971. Janet, known as Jean, was an Ashburton girl and a widow, following a short-lived marriage to Charles Cecil Maguire. They had wed in 1913, and he had died in 1916, aged but 33. Jean was some ten years older than Nugget, and they had no children. The 1935 Electoral Roll has Jean and Alex living at 154 Sidney Street, Wellington, and Nugget's last season with Pastimes was in 1936–37, but the couple then moved south and in 1938 were at 346 High St, Dunedin West.

In 1939 'Racket' ('Rapid Rise in Rugby') wrote: 'Today he is employed at Dunedin's Chief Post Office, being just as popular in his official capacity as he was in his playing days. He has also figured in senior cricket in Dunedin as a member of the Kaikorai eleven … both in the senior and intermediate grades.'

On 24 February 1941, still in Dunedin but now resident at 118 Stafford Street, Nugget enlisted in the armed forces. In his Attestation he gave his occupation as 'Custodian C.P.O.', and his preferred 'arm of service' was 'Infantry A.S.C.'. He wrote that he had served three years in the Territorials, 'service completed'. We do not know where or when this might have been, but given the family legend that he joined the army to get fit for rugby and earnt his nickname because, as a consequence, his boots were always highly polished, this may have been in his early Wellington years. The Army measured him as: 'Height 6 feet 5 1/2 inches, Weight 14 stone 0 pounds, Chest expanded 43 1/2 inches, Range 5 1/2 inches.' He was found to have 'moderate degree varicose veins Rt leg below knee' (was this the one he broke?) and 'extra-systoles' and was placed in Grade Two. At the time his chest X-ray was clear.

He went into camp in B.T.D., Wingatui, Dunedin, on 9 July 1942, and earned early promotion, becoming 'T/Sgt while on Inst. Staff at Wingatui' on 14 October that year. While serving there he had time for –

One Final Sporting Achievement

On 5 March 1943 the *New Zealand Free Lance* reported, in an article entitled '"Nugget" Pringle Takes All 10 Wickets':

> Playing for an Army team in the intermediate grade the other Saturday, A. ('Nugget') Pringle took all 10 Kaikorai wickets at a cost of 41 runs. Six of his victims were clean-bowled, three were caught, and one was dismissed l.b.w. 'Nugget' is better known as a Wellington representative Rugby player for several years and as a fine line-out forward in the New Zealand team of 1923. But for an injury he probably would have gained a place in the All Black team that visited Great Britain in 1924. Pringle played senior cricket for the Kaikorai Club before he joined the forces and he was a more than useful bowler. It is more than likely that he will take in hand the coaching of one of the Army Rugby teams in the coming season.

But it was not to be – in Dunedin at least. In April 1943 he was transferred to 'Unit & R.T.D. Instr. Crs. Dist. School', Burnham Military Camp, south of Christchurch, and there he remained, gaining promotion to T/S/Sgt on 1 August 1944, and 'Conducting Warrant duties' during 19–21 February 1945. Then illness struck.

In August 1946 he gave a 12-month history of productive cough and weight loss of over a stone, and a chest X-ray revealed Pulmonary Tuberculosis, with cavitation (i.e., a cavity in the lung resulting from tuberculous destruction of lung tissue) on the left. Described as 'tall and thin', and now down to 13 stone, he was a very sick boy, and, in retrospect, looked more than a little gaunt in a photograph taken as he marched at the head of his unit in November 1945. He was placed in Grade Four, 100% disabled for two years at least, and admitted to hospital, later being transferred to Cashmere Sanatorium. The doctors deemed his illness, while not directly attributable to conditions of service, to have been 'aggravated (by) Climate and living conditions in Camp and overwork'.

On 30 January 1947 his condition was 'much improved … [g]etting up a few hours daily', which gives some indication of how sick he had been. On 12 March 1947, with the rank of W.O II, he was granted a medical discharge and pension. This, in addition to a lump sum that, when he was still adjudged 100% disabled on 1 April 1950, amounted to 70/- (70 shillings) per week. Later, he was awarded the War Medal 1939–45 and the NZ War Service Medal.

And a Final Tribute

On 10 September 1966 the *Evening Post* published an anonymous article entitled 'Millard Team of Stars from Rugby's Earlier Days'. In it Mr J.N. Millard, the 'Professor of Rugby' of 1927, selected what he considered to be the best team of players who had represented Wellington in his years as a selector (i.e., 1927–33 and 1952–53). All but two had worn the silver fern, and all but three were from his earlier years. His team was:

> **Evening Post.**
>
> H.R. Pollock (Petone, 1929–39)
> W.L. Elvy (Petone, 1927–29), A.E. Cooke (Hutt, 1930), R.A. Jarden (University, 1949–56)
> M.F. Nicholls (Petone, 1920–31), L.M. Johnson (Wellington, 1923–32)
> F.D. Kilby (Wellington, 1927–35)
> C.G. Porter (Wellington College Old Boys and Athletic, 1917–18 and 1923–30)
> W.H. Clarke (University, 1950–56), E.F. Barry (Wellington, 1926–36), W. Peck,[1] (Hutt, 1927–33) **or** A. Pringle (Oriental, 1922–27), H.F. McLean (Wellington, 1928–33)
> E.M. Jessep (Poneke, 1926–32), A. Lambourn (Petone, 1932–36), B.J. Lloyd (Wellington, 1946–53)

The article added: 'Mr Millard has named an alternative for the lock positions, emphasising that selecting this side would create some difficulty, as players in his earlier term played under the 2-3-2 scrum system. "We would have to train the locks to play in the 3-4-1 scrum," he said.'

---

1 This is the self-same Peck who Nugget was picked to oppose in that last fateful club game in 1929. Curious that two such strong players should have found themselves playing in B team matches – not once but twice – stacking the decks, one might think!

CHAPTER 14

Recovery, Reunions, Retirement

Forty years younger than his Christchurch uncle, the author grew up in Wellington. The families seldom travelled and met infrequently. His first memory of his uncle is as a small boy on a family visit to Alex and Jean for afternoon tea in their Christchurch home at 90 Harewood Road in the late 1940s or thereabouts. He recalls attractive and spotless surroundings and a warm and happy environment, but his abiding memory is of the need for hygiene – handwashing, separate towels and separate crockery, for fear of contagion. At the time Nugget was something of an enforced recluse.

On a less formal and happier occasion in the early 1950s he sat with his uncle, now recovered, on the Terrace at Wellington College watching the First XI play. To his nephew, Uncle Alex was a principled, but nonetheless warm, smiling, kind and generous man, who laughed readily, and for 30 years sent his nephews unsolicited, and one fears not uncommonly unacknowledged, First Day Covers, addressed in his splendid bold flowing script. These were mostly of Health Stamps, appropriately enough, as the first issued in 1929 and 1930 were to 'Help Stamp Out Tuberculosis'.

Once recovered, Nugget was able to enjoy his later years, and was an active member of the Canterbury Cricket Supporters

Club. He returned to Wellington on occasion for family functions and reunions, including the Wellington Rugby Football Union's Old-Timers Days in October 1952 and September 1964, and, most importantly, the Oriental Football Club's 75th Jubilee, Easter 1963. This splendid occasion began with a reception on the Friday at the gymnasium (ladies welcome). On the Saturday morning the delegates marched from the railway station to the Cenotaph where a wreath was laid, then, still before lunch, paraded from Wellington South Intermediate School to Athletic Park for the official welcome by the club president. Light lunch and refreshments (at last!!) were followed by Oriental schoolboy games, a past player's game, and at 3.00 p.m. the annual season opener between Oriental and Kaierau (Wanganui). In the evening a dinner was held at the Athletic Club's gymnasium (sorry, no ladies). The Sunday featured an all-day picnic at Maidstone Park (reached by train), while on the Monday an afternoon match between Oriental and St Pat's Old Boys was followed in the evening by a ball at the Majestic Cabaret. How Nugget must have enjoyed that event, perhaps with Jean, and in all probability in the company of his two brothers.

The Unluckiest All Black?

Clearly Nugget was in no way as unfortunate as men like Gallaher and Carson who lost their lives in the world wars, nor, perhaps, some of those whose playing careers were ended prematurely by devastating injury or illness. Nonetheless, purely in terms of All Black appearances, was there ever a man unluckier than one who, through injury and affliction and sheer mischance, together with the timing of trials and the vagaries of selection, missed out, by a whisker, on two home internationals and three overseas tours? This is not to suggest that Nugget ever displayed any rancour or sense of grievance relating to these matters. He gave his all for the game he loved, and enjoyed doing so, and that was that. The first All Black cap, after all, is the one that matters most, and for that he was, and always will be, known as Alex 'Nugget' Pringle – the All Black.

Nugget was to outlive Jean by two years, dying in Christchurch on 21 February 1973. He is at rest with Jean in Ruru Lawn Cemetery, Christchurch. On 23 February 1973, this obituary appeared in the *Wellington Evening Post*:

Evening Post.

Former Rugby Star Dies

CHRISTCHURCH, Today (PA). Mr Alexander Pringle, who died in Christchurch this week, was a 1923 All Black.

Known as 'Nugget' Pringle, he was an outstanding rugby forward, whose exceptional height, 6ft 5½in, made him a tremendous force in the line-outs.

As a member of the Oriental Club, he played for Wellington from 1922 to 1927, and represented New Zealand in a Test against New South Wales at Lancaster Park in 1923.

He also played for the North Island in 1923 and 1924. Mr Pringle would have been a top contender for selection in the 1924-25 Invincibles, but injury blighted his chances. In later life Mr Pringle settled in Christchurch.

Bibliography

Anonymous (1966). 'Millard Team of Stars from Rugby's Earlier Days', *Evening Post*, 10 September.

Brownlie, Laurie (undated). Player Profiles Prepared for the New Zealand Rugby Museum. Palmerston North: Rugby Museum Society of New Zealand.

Dominion (cuttings from various issues).

Evening Post (various issues). Archives. Wellington: National Library of New Zealand

Fleming, Tom (August 1960) 'Tom Fleming on Rugby', Cutting from an unknown newspaper.

Growden, Greg (2010). *Inside the Wallabies: The Real Story – The Players, The Politics, The Games from 1908 to Today*. Crows Nest NSW: Allen & Unwin.

Hutt News, 8 August 1929. Archives. Wellington: National Library of New Zealand.

Jennings, A.A. (1935). *Souvenir of the Wellington Mercantile Cricket League (Inc.) 1921 to 1935: Activities, Hints, Records, etc*. Wellington: Ferguson & Osborne.

Knight, Lindsay (undated). Player Profiles Prepared for the New Zealand Rugby Museum. Palmerston North: Rugby Museum Society of New Zealand.

Luxford, Bob (undated). Player Profiles Prepared for the New Zealand Rugby Museum. Palmerston North: Rugby Museum Society of New Zealand.

New Zealand Army Service Records. Available online at: https://www.govt.nz/browse/history-culture-and-heritage/nz-history/military-history-records-and-medals/.
New Zealand Free Lance (cuttings from various issues).
New Zealand Rugby Museum (NZRM) website: http://rugbymuseum.co.nz
New Zealand Sportsman (cuttings from various issues).
New Zealand Times (cuttings from various issues).
Noble-Campbell, Gordon, et al. (2019). *Ghost Rugby Clubs of Wellington*. Glenbeigh Books.
NZ Truth (various issues). Archives. Wellington: National Library of New Zealand.
Oriental Rugby Football Club (ORFC) (undated). *Annual Report*. Wellington: ORFC.
Oxford University Press (1979). *Oxford English Dictionary, Compact Edition*. Oxford: Oxford University Press.
Oxford University Press (1997). *Oxford Dictionary of New Zealand English*. Wellington: Oxford University Press.
Partridge, Eric (1937). *A Dictionary of Slang and Unconventional English*. London: Macmillan & Co.
Racket (1939). 'Rapid Rise in Rugby: From Junior to All Black in Two Seasons. "Nugget" Pringle's Career: Post-War Impressions of Wellington Player', *Evening Star* (sports special edition), June.
Sport (cuttings from various issues).
Timaru Herald (various issues). Archives. Wellington: National Library of New Zealand
Wikipedia (n.d.) '1923 Waratahs tour of NZ'. Available online at: https://www.google.com/url?sa=t&rct=j&q=&esrc=s&source=web&cd=&ved=2ahUKEwigjpmItuTuAhW-QEEAHc9PAmcQFjABegQIAxAC&url=https%3A%2F%2Fen.wikipedia.org%2Fwiki%2F1923_Waratahs_tour_of_New_Zealand&usg=AOvVaw1dX_6XmJzs42FowzYZgXrN

About the Author

Wellington born and bred and an Otago graduate, Bob Pringle elected, over 50 years ago, to pursue his orthopaedic surgical career in England. With him went his son Chris, and in England they stayed, Bob in Shrewsbury, Chris now in Oxford.

Together they remain true Kiwis at heart, and avid supporters of the All Blacks and Black Caps – which still leaves room for Warwickshire and Worcestershire cricket, and the Northampton Saints.